The Literary Essay
Analyzing Craft and Theme

Kate Roberts and Katy Wischow

LUCY CALKINS, SERIES EDITOR

Photography by Peter Cunningham

HEINEMANN ◆ PORTSMOUTH, NH

This unit within the information writing progression

GRADE 6

In *The Literary Essay*, students craft essays that make arguments about characters and themes, learning strategies essayists use to gather, analyze, and explain evidence from the text to support their claims.

GRADE 7

In *The Art of Argument*, students learn to write essays that build convincing, nuanced arguments, balancing evidence and analysis to persuade readers to shift their beliefs or take action.

THIS UNIT

GRADE 8

In *The Literary Essay*, students write arguments and counterarguments about themes in texts, supporting their positions with details of plot, character and author's craft.

This unit within the grade 8 progression

UNIT 1

In *Investigative Journalism*, students learn to use sharp observations of life to write news and investigative articles about meaningful topics, crafting vivid narratives and elaborating multiple perspectives.

THIS UNIT

UNIT 2

In *The Literary Essay*, students write arguments and counterarguments about themes in texts, supporting their positions with details of plot, character, and author's craft.

UNIT 3

In *Position Papers*, students learn ways writers explain complex issues and compose arguments by drawing on evidence, contextualizing their positions, and addressing multiple perspectives.

This book is dedicated to Maggie, for being the strongest reason that my claim, "life is awesome," is true.

—Kate

This book is dedicated to Jane & Harold and to Russ & Doris.

—Katy

DEDICATED TO TEACHERS™

*first*hand
An imprint of Heinemann
361 Hanover Street
Portsmouth, NH 03801–3912
www.heinemann.com

Offices and agents throughout the world

© 2014 by Kate Roberts and Katy Wischow

The authors and publisher wish to thank those who have generously given permission to reprint borrowed material:

Excerpts from "All Summer in a Day" by Ray Bradbury. Copyright © 1954, renewed 1982 by Ray Bradbury. Reprinted by permission of Don Congdon Associates, Inc.

Excerpts from "If Only We Had Taller Been" by Ray Bradbury. Copyright © 1973 by Ray Bradbury. Reprinted by permission of Don Congdon Associates, Inc.

Cataloging-in-Publication data is on file with the Library of Congress.

ISBN-13: 978-0-325-05950-1

Production: Elizabeth Valway, David Stirling, and Abigail Heim
Cover and interior designs: Jenny Jensen Greenleaf
Series photographs by Peter Cunningham and Nadine Baldasare
Composition: Publishers' Design and Production Services, Inc.
Manufacturing: Steve Bernier

Printed in the United States of America on acid-free paper
18 17 16 15 14 PAH 1 2 3 4 5

Acknowledgments

IT IS A STRANGE FEELING to see your name on the cover of a book—you are so keenly aware that the pages you hold in your hand would never have materialized without an army of people working together. We are so grateful for the army of educators and editors that worked to make this book happen.

This book stands on the shoulders of all the teachers, students, books, leaders, colleagues, and classrooms that have formed the foundation for the ideas, lessons, and methods we outline here. Just as the eighth-graders in these pages succeed by drawing on their whole community of teaching and learning, this book could not have been written in isolation. The legacy of thinking and teaching that we lean on here is humbling. In particular, of course, we have been shaped by the thinking and discussion of the Teachers College Reading and Writing Project and the educators who have been influenced by its work.

This book, like so many others, simply would not exist without the contributions of teachers and schools. In particular, Theresa Walter and her eighth-grade students in Great Neck, New York, dove into this unit with commitment and enthusiasm; their feedback is threaded throughout most every lesson here. Many thanks to Ms. Walter for her sense of humor and her thoughtfulness, and thanks, too, to her beautiful students for their hard work and honest input. We also thank Aneal Alston, who graciously supported our work in the school building he leads. Other teachers helped us along the way, and we would like to thank Leah Bragin and Lindsay Powell at School of the Future in Manhattan, as well as Leigh-Anne Hawkins at Knollwood School in Fair Haven, New Jersey, for being willing to come in and try out some lessons in a pinch. Thanks are also due to the schools and classrooms in which we have worked and learned for years. Our thinking in this book has been shaped and reshaped by our experiences in schools across the globe.

In addition to the work within schools, we have been so greatly helped and influenced by our colleagues at the Teachers College Reading and Writing Project. It is impossible to overstate the effect Lucy Calkins has had on our teaching—she is the Gandalf to our Frodo, the Dumbledore to our Hermione. We would not be who we are or where we are without her relentless work ethic and wide, wise vision. And in this book, she was far more than editor—working on every page, through many drafts, and providing us with others to help as well.

Kathleen Tolan has been a vital guide in our education, pushing us to think in more rigorous ways about kids and learning and supporting us as we faced the challenges of our careers. And Mary Ehrenworth has been a constant light—showing us the way up ahead on the path where she has already sprinted, and keeping our spirits high. Amanda Hartman, too, gets our gratitude for her support and leadership. Our leaders have truly led us, even in confusing times, and for that we are grateful. We have also been fed (literally and figuratively) by the staff developers we work with at the Project. In particular we owe thanks to Colleen Cruz, for her friendship and wise counsel, Brooke Geller, for reminding us to focus on the positive in every situation, and Audra Kirshbaum Robb for her intelligence and ability to craft the perfect joke. Some of our colleagues' contributions are visible in the pages of this book; we cannot thank Marjorie Martinelli and Liz Dunford enough for their contributions. We thank all of our colleagues for their tireless work and generous spirits—you will not find a better group of hardworking people than these folks. They are an inspiration.

Huge thanks to Felicia O'Brien, who was an always-positive, always-dedicated presence during the process of writing the book, and who offered invaluable support in problem-solving and revising. We will miss messaging you at 5 AM. Thanks, too, to Jenny Bender who stepped in to contribute vital help when we needed it. We are also beyond grateful to Abby Heim who has managed the complex process of turning words on a computer screen into the bound book you hold in your hands. The team at Heinemann is a special crew—they managed to push us to think in better and better ways for kids— all while moving the project along. And, of course, Kate Montgomery is the guiding light of this team, ever reminding us to place students in the forefront of our minds. We cannot imagine working with a better team. Thank you.

Finally, we would like to thank our wives, Maggie and Desi, for not throwing things at us when we woke up at 4:30 AM for the thousandth time, or stayed up later than seemed normal to write. Thank you for being flexible with schedules, for listening to us rehearse and whine and gloat, for believing we could do it when we weren't sure ourselves. Thank you for your constant love and your good, good hearts.

The class described in this unit is a composite class, with children and partnerships of children gleaned from classrooms in very different contexts, then put together here. We wrote the units this way to bring you a wide array of wonderful, quirky, various children and also to illustrate for you the predictable (and unpredictable) situations and responses this unit has created in classrooms around the nation and world.

—Kate and Katy

Contents

Acknowledgments • iii

Welcome to the Unit • vii

BEND I   The Thematic Essay

1. Looking for Themes All around Us . . . • 2

In this session, you'll remind students that writers are on the lookout for themes in all of the texts they read, and are able to explain, with details from the text, why they believe that theme to be present.

2. Reading Closely to Develop Themes • 14

In this session, you'll teach students that academic writers look closely at a text to further develop their understanding of the text's themes, and then use writing to discover what the whole text is saying about those ideas.

3. Fine-Tuning Themes by Studying Author's Craft • 25

In this session, you'll teach students that when analyzing a text, literary essayists pay attention to the details of the plot and character development as well as the author's crafting decisions, reflecting on the connection between the author's message and his or her craft.

4. Drafting Essays • 36

In this session, you'll teach students that when getting ready to draft, writers recall what they already know about the genre they are writing in, as well as examine mentor texts in that genre, to make a plan and set goals for their writing.

5. Finding the Courage to Revise Your Thinking • 46

In this session, you'll teach students that essay writers often have to stop at the end of a draft and ask themselves—are all of my original ideas still true? Is there anything I should change? If so, writers then have the courage to revise their thinking.

6. Clarifying Relationships between Evidence and Ideas • 55

In this session, you'll teach students that essayists can use logic, specifically logical sentence frames, to help them clarify the relationship between their evidence and their ideas.

7. Counterargument within Literary Essays • 65

In this session, you'll teach students that essayists look for places where there could be another interpretation or opinion about the text, and they write to try and argue why their interpretation is the best one, by nodding to the alternative argument and then explaining why that one is not as sound.

8. Editing Using All You Know • 75

In this session, you could teach students that writers use all they know and all they have (relying on the resources at their disposal) to put the final touches on their drafts, and that they continue to look for ways to outgrow themselves, this time by lifting the level of their conventions.

BEND II The Author's Craft Essay

9. Noticing How an Author Tends to Write • 82

In this session, you'll teach students that literary essayists look for craft moves that the author uses repeatedly. Then, essayists write a bit about why they think the author chooses to write in that way, and what effect those craft moves have on the text.

10. The Power of Symbolism • 92

In this session, you'll teach students that literary essayists are often on the lookout for one especially powerful craft move that authors use to great effect—symbols. You will teach students to look for this device in their own texts and to write long to discover the deeper meaning behind the symbols they discover.

11. Planning the Author's Craft Essay • 100

In this session, you could teach students that writers of author's craft essays pause and plan how their craft essays will go, and that when they do this they have to choose whether to focus in deeply on one craft move or whether to instead analyze a few they see in the text.

12. Framing Essays with Relevance and Context: Introductions and Conclusions • 107

In this session, you'll teach students that essayists write introductions that explain the text being analyzed and the greater relevance of their essays. They often conclude their essays by leaving their readers with their most powerful thoughts.

13. Adopting an Essayist's Tone • 116

In this session, you'll teach students that writers can adopt an essayist's engaging and formal tone by varying their sentence length and using sophisticated language.

14. A Comma Inquiry • 124

In this session, you could teach students that writers use the comma in multiple ways to make their writing readable, engaging, and strong.

BEND III The Comparative Essay

15. Writing across Texts • 130

In this session, you'll teach students that literary essayists often write as a way to think about more than one text at a time, pushing themselves to do the work of comparing and contrasting similar ideas across different texts.

16. Writing Comparative Essays on Demand • 141

In this session, you'll teach students that writers have to use all that they know about essays to write not just well, but also quickly and with flexibility.

17. Publishing on the Internet • 149

In this session, you could teach students that writers decide where on the Internet they want to publish a portion of their pieces, and then work to make their writing Internet ready.

Welcome to the Unit

THIS UNIT STRIVES TO HELP you to lead your students to become more independent with the essay-writing skills they have acquired across their elementary- and middle-school years while also teaching new, high-leverage strategies that will help your young writers meet and exceed the expectations of their high school communities.

To meet both of these goals—independence and rigor—this unit will take you and your students through three incarnations of an essay. First, they will write an essay based on a theme of a text. Next, they will push themselves to write an essay analyzing an author's writing craft. Finally, in a short series of lessons, you will help your students apply what they have learned to write an essay comparing two texts, one of which they will bring to the table from their own reading past. Each essay calls for students to hold on to what they have learned before while also pushing their writing and thinking forward. You will spend time modeling your own thinking and writing, and you will coach students to develop strong claims about the texts they are reading. You will confer and pull aside small groups in response to your students' needs, and your classroom will be overflowing with well-crafted mentor essays and useful charts—all to teach your students that writing literary essays is a skill that they can improve upon no matter what level they begin at, no matter what teaching they have had in the past.

As you teach your students to write more powerfully about the texts they are reading, you will also, even if inadvertently, teach them to be more powerful readers. At the start of each *bend* or phase of the unit, there are a few lessons that ask your students to reflect upon and analyze, in complex and sophisticated ways, the texts they are reading. While the explicit purpose of these lessons is to help your students to collect ideas and thinking for their future essays, they also serve to deepen the reading experienced in your classroom, and to give your students new ways to see more in the texts they read.

When this unit is over and you move on to the next, you will teach your students how to write position papers about a controversial issue. Students will live purely in the land of argumentative writing—where they will need to *prove* their thinking, not just support it, and where they will need to practice the critical skill of considering the counterargument at every turn. Here, in this unit, you will be revisiting many of the foundational moves of essay writing that are like argument writing—in the writing there are claims, with supports and evidence. But literary essays live a bit in both worlds—the world of information, or explanatory, writing and the world of argument writing. While, on the one hand, a literary essay is like an argument in structure, it is a little bit less of an argument than its cousin, the research-based argument essay. That is to say, when your writers posit that a character embodies a certain trait, it is unlikely that someone who has read that same story will say, "No, that character certainly does *not* embody that trait." And so, here we treat literary essay as an essay in form and skill but with less pressure on the writer to argue a point as to support it—a perfect unit for your students at this time of the year.

OVERVIEW OF THE UNIT

You will begin the unit in what is most likely comfortable territory—teaching your students to write about and reflect upon the themes they see in the texts they have chosen to write about. Urging students to use their prior learning, you will push them to collect a few possible themes and to write long about them in their notebooks, using their writing partners for support. Then you will teach your students to read their texts a little more closely, paying attention to the small details in critical scenes to help them refine their thinking about the themes they originally named. In an effort to push the sophistication and nuance of both their thinking and their reading of their texts, you will then teach students to focus on theme by paying attention to the author's craft of the text, using that craft to unlock more of the author's purpose.

In the next part of Bend I, you will coach your students to use all that they know to draft their first essay of the unit. In particular, you will offer your students a mentor essay to study for ways to get started and then to keep going as they draft. This work encourages independence, assuming that most of your class has written many essays before and will not need you to outline every step, bit by bit, for them. In addition, it gives students a vision for what a draft of their literary essay should look like. While the draft you show them will not have bells and whistles yet, (you will add these into your writing as you go), it will be a high bar for your class to reach on this day.

After their drafts are written, you will teach your students a few high-leverage, sophisticated strategies to help lift the level of their essays. First, you will encourage students to be critical of their own writing, and to look for places where their essays are not making sense, modeling the skill and the courage it takes writers to fix problems as they arise. You will also teach students to use logical reasoning to clarify the relationship between their evidence and the ideas in their essays. Then you will ask your students to search for any alternative arguments that could be made about the texts they are analyzing, and to speak back to those alternatives in their own essays. Finally, you will ask your students to edit their essays to the best of their abilities, being sure to pull aside small groups and conferences to help students understand ways to make their writing all the more powerful, correct, and readable.

As students finish their first essays, you will rally them to focus on another in Bend II. This time, though, you will teach students that powerful readers focus not only on the themes that tend to emerge in a text, but also on the craft that an author tends to use as he or she writes. This focus on the patterns of craft that we see as we read pushes your students to think about the text as something that a person—the author—has created purposefully, and that the choices he or she tends to make around word choice, syntax or literary devices, matter. Of course, you will also point out that oddities matter as well and deserve to be studied, and you will teach that there is value in taking note of the symbols an author has layered within the text.

As students plan and draft this second essay, you will focus on teaching them ways that writers refine their introductions and conclusions so that these provide the context that readers will need in order to enter the world of the essayist and so that the essay topic will feel relevant to the readers' world

and to their own lives. In addition, you will teach students ways that writers adopt the tone of an essayist, paying close attention to the language they use and making sure that it matches their intent. In this bend you will ask that students reflect upon and hold onto the lessons they learned in Bend I, and you'll push them to think and write in more sophisticated ways.

Finally, in Bend III, a "mini-bend" of two power-packed sessions, you will ask your students to use all that they have learned both this year and in years past to conceive of and draft an essay in which they compare and contrast the themes of two texts. One of these texts will be the one they have chosen to write about across the unit. The other will be a different text of their choosing. This work asks students to apply what they know to a slightly different task: to decide how a compare-and-contrast essay might be the same and different from the work they have done so far and to write one, both with minimal teaching from you. This is an apt way to end your unit, as it will most clearly reflect the way in which your students will write in high school.

ASSESSMENT

Knowing that one of your challenges in this unit will be to avoid unnecessary re-teaching and instead set students up for greater and greater independence in literary analysis and powerful writing, assessment at the start of the unit is crucial. Some teachers begin the year with on-demand assessments of narrative, argument, and informational writing, while some choose to assess only one kind at a time, a day or so before the unit begins. Whenever you choose to conduct this on-demand assessment, you won't want it to feel like busywork or like a high-stakes exam. Rather, it should feel like an opportunity for students to show off to you what they've learned over the years and for them to help make sure that they are getting the teaching that is best suited to them.

In this unit you will teach students to consider some of the alternative interpretations of texts, and to incorporate these alternatives into their essays; however, literary essays are not exactly arguments. In many ways they are informational/explanatory—"Here are some themes in this text, let me explain them." But literary essays do not exactly fit with what we have come to know about informational writing either. And so here we treat literary essay as an essay in form and skill but with less pressure on writers to argue their point as much as support it—and we recommend using the on-demand prompt for argument writing. We suggest you use the argument progression and set of tools because, while a literary essay is not a perfect example of an argument and it shares many of the qualities of informational writing, the structure and skills within a literary essay most closely align with the argument progression and the Common Core State Standards for argument writing.

We have provided you with instruments—learning progressions, rubrics, checklists, and leveled exemplar texts—that will help you to see where, in the trajectory of writing development, each of your students lie. These tools will help you to name some of the next steps for your students, and will help you—and your students—see their growth as writers. We suggest you begin with the following on-demand prompt for argument writing from the book, *Writing Pathways: Performance Assessments and Learning Progressions, Grades 6–8,* included in this series:

"Think of a topic or issue you care about, an issue around which you have a very strong opinion. Tomorrow, you will have forty-five minutes to write an essay in which you will write your opinion or claim and argue why it is right, telling reasons why you feel that way. When you do this, draw on everything you know about essays. If you want to find and use information from a book or another outside source, you may bring that with you tomorrow. Please keep in mind that you'll have forty-five minutes to complete this, so you will need to plan, draft, revise and edit in one sitting. In your writing, make sure you:

- Write an introduction
- State your claim
- Give reasons and evidence
- Organize your writing
- Acknowledge counterclaims
- Use transition words
- Write a conclusion."

Whether you give this assessment at the start of the year or a short while before this unit, you will want to give yourself enough time to examine your students' work and notice patterns and trends. You will want to assess where each student falls on the Learning Progression for Argument Writing. You might start by reading each student's work, comparing it to the exemplar texts in the progression. Don't worry too much about whether a piece of work precisely matches each descriptor at a level—few essays will perfectly align to a single level. Look for where most of your students fall, using that knowledge to inform your plans for the unit.

This assessment work is powerful to do in collaboration with colleagues, so that you are aligning your expectations and understandings of student work across the school. You might also consider sharing the process you're using, or the trends you're spotting, with your students. The progression and other assessment tools are powerful for you, but can be even more powerful when students use them to set their own goals and next steps.

GETTING READY

To begin, you will need to be sure that your students have writer's notebooks and writing partners. These will be resources for your students across the unit. Their notebooks will be places for them to collect their ideas and plan their essays, yes, but they will also be a refuge for students when they want to try something out in their writing but are not yet ready to commit it to the draft. As you will see as you begin reading this unit, your students' writing partners will be lifelines for them almost every day that they write. We lean on writing partners at every turn for a number of reasons. First, we see talk as an essential tool for writers—to discuss, rehearse, and celebrate. But also, when looking ahead to high school, your students will want to know how to use their classmates to help them with tough assignments. The community you create this year in your eighth-grade classroom will ripple out into the ways that your students help each other in the years to come.

You will also want to gather examples of literary essays written by eighth-graders in your community. Nothing beats the ability to say, "Here are the essays last year's class wrote. You can do this too." We provide examples on the CD-ROM, but the most engaging examples will come from your own students or students of fellow teachers.

You will see that in this unit we center our work on Ray Bradbury's "All Summer in a Day," and while we find this story to be a highly effective and engaging mentor text for eighth-graders, we encourage you to find another text that is a better fit for your students if you feel it is necessary. Similarly, while in this unit we suggest that students read dystopian novels for their independent work, and we suggest titles that have worked in our classrooms, you might make a different choice. We very much hope that you will be sure that the texts your students read for this unit fit your purposes and their interests. Some teachers have chosen to focus on historical fiction, while others have chosen to stick with dystopia, but to give their students short stories, not novels (we offer some suggestions for dystopian short stories in the unit as well). Whatever choice you make, be sure that your class has had a chance to read the texts they will be writing about ahead of time, before your writing unit begins.

Looking for Themes
All around Us . . .

IN THIS SESSION, you'll remind students that writers are on the lookout for themes in all of the texts they read, and are able to explain, with details from the text, why they believe that theme to be present.

GETTING READY

✔ Before starting the session, partners will need to have agreed upon a book (or conceivably a short story) they both know well that will be the focus of their literary essay writing throughout the unit. Students will need these texts throughout the unit.

✔ Partners need to be sitting alongside each other during the minilesson and work time, throughout the unit.

✔ A video clip of a song in which theme can be inferred or discussed. We use Taylor Swift's "Safe and Sound" http://www.youtube.com/watch?v=RzhAS_ GnJIc (YouTube search term "Safe and Sound Taylor Swift"). If this is hard to do, plan an alternative (see Connection).

✔ "How to Write a Thematic Essay" anchor chart, with the first bullet and subpoints already written (see Teaching).

✔ Copies of the class-shared anchor text, "All Summer in a Day" by Ray Bradbury, one per student. Students should be familiar with this text prior to today's session (see Teaching and Active Engagement).

✔ Your own writer's notebook. Be prepared to write an entry on the theme of the class anchor text "All Summer in a Day" or have that entry already written (see Teaching).

✔ Chart paper and markers to create the "Prompts to Push Writers to Speculate about Themes in a Text" chart (see Mid-Workshop Teaching).

COMMON CORE STATE STANDARDS: W.8.1, W.8.3.b, W.8.4, W.8.6, W.8.9.a, W.8.10, RL.8.1, RL.8.2, RL.8.3, RL.8.4, SL.8.1, SL.8.2, L.8.1, L.8.2, L.8.3

AT THE START OF THIS UNIT, you stand at a crossroads with your eighth-graders. (Picture a desert scene, sky for miles, and you standing at the center of four corners stretching out endlessly on the horizon.) Behind them lies all that they have learned about essay writing, about literary essays specifically, and about reading in powerful ways. Ahead of them lies high school and college, a virtual sea of essays about texts. And here you stand, about to begin joining what your students have been taught in the past with what will be expected of them in the future. It can make you a bit breathless, if you think on it for too long.

By the end of the first bend, your class will have written their first literary essay of this unit. This first essay will focus on analyzing the theme of a text—either a short story or a novel. You will encourage them to use all that they have learned in their past schooling to write the most effective and powerful essays they are able to write, and along the way you will teach them some new ways to make their writing that much better.

But this bend and this unit also aim to help your students—who are standing there with you at that crossroads—take in the view around them. This can be tough. Like a teenager who has his eyes glued to his smart phone while visiting the Grand Canyon, eighth-graders sometimes forget to reflect on what they have learned, and they sometimes miss the big picture. Sometimes we do too, for that matter. So this bend strives to help you and your classes to move forward in their literary essay-writing journey while also looking back for lessons from the past.

These first few sessions focus on helping your eighth-graders identify and analyze the themes of a text. While much of this work might live in the reading component of your curriculum, here you will teach students that *writing* about the themes in texts can help them to clarify, support, and complicate their thinking. To begin, you will teach your students that they are surrounded by themed texts—certainly within the printed texts they read, but also in the songs they listen to, the shows they watch, even the games they play. You will remind your students that identifying the theme in all those texts involves stepping back and asking, "What is this text really saying about some of the topics it addresses?" and you will remind them that they can use writing to grow those initial ideas into something more sophisticated.

As we mentioned in the Welcome to the Unit, before this unit begins, your students will need to have already read the texts that they will be analyzing. The unit will work equally well whether your students are writing about short stories or novels, but we recommend the latter. Each choice has its own

---

"You will teach students that writing about the themes in texts can help them clarify, support, and complicate their thinking."

---

rewards and challenges. It is easier to absorb the entirety of a short text and to find the passages to mine, but there is much more to write about in a novel, making the experience of writing about novels more forgiving and generative. For example, it is easier to find support for a theme when writing about a novel than a short story, and easier to find patterns in the craft moves an author has used. Whichever you choose, be sure your students have already finished reading the texts they are writing about before the start of this unit since this is a writing unit. Students will do some rereading during the sessions, but there is not time within these sessions for them to actually read a novel.

Additionally, you will want your students to have at least one person in the class who is writing about the same text, and the two people who share a text should be partners, sitting alongside each other throughout the unit during both the mini-lesson and work time. You may achieve this by first partnering

students and then asking the twosomes to decide on a book they have both read and cared about. You may, instead, ask students to each suggest a short list of texts they'd like to write about and then use those suggestions to form same-book partnerships. You may have more than one set of partners writing about a particular text, in which case the foursomes can be called clubs and can meet together some of the time.

In the unit, the class will also need to have read (or heard you read aloud) the short story that threads its way throughout. That story is Ray Bradbury's "All Summer in a Day," chosen because of its brevity as well as its depth. This is a dystopian text. Dystopia is both engaging to most adolescents as well as rife with theme. We've included a short list of favorites from this genre in case you want to set students up, well before the unit, to read one of these texts with their partner in preparation for the unit. However, your students do not need to read from this genre since the genre choice in no way shapes this unit. If you decide to highlight dystopian texts, these are a few texts that eighth-graders have especially loved: "Harrison Bergeron," by Kurt Vonnegut, "The Invasion from Outer Space," by Steven Millhauser, "The Veldt," by Ray Bradbury, or stories from the anthology *Brave New Worlds*, edited by John Joseph Adams or *After*, edited by Ellen Datlow and Terri Windling. If your students are choosing dystopian novels, they might read *The Knife of Never Letting Go*, by Patrick Ness, *Divergent*, by Veronica Roth, *The Maze Runner*, by James Dashner, or of course *The Hunger Games*, by Suzanne Collins.

In any case, your students need to enter this session sitting alongside a same-book partner, and those partners need to have completed the book and to have copies with them. The class also needs to have read, or heard you read, "All Summer in a Day." You could substitute a different text for that one, but we do not recommend that for your first experience teaching the unit, since our work with this short story threads through the entire unit.

Looking for Themes All around Us . . .

CONNECTION

Play a video of a current popular song or artist. Point out that songs, like stories, have themes or lessons that the songwriter and singer are trying to get across. Channel students to discuss in partners what the song's theme might be.

"Writers, I have to admit something to you. Yesterday I was coming to work, and a song came on, and it was one of those things—I don't know if it was the song, or what was in my heart, or if I was tired, but I totally choked up. And—this is the part that is tough to admit here—the thing is, it was to a Taylor Swift song." The class erupted in laughs. I nodded solemnly. "That's right. I'm a Taylor Swift fan. Here is the song that struck me." I played a minute of a YouTube video of the Taylor Swift song, "Safe and Sound" (http://www.youtube.com/watch?v=RzhAS_GnJIc, YouTube search term "Safe and Sound Taylor Swift").

"I was thinking about it later, and I think what got to me was what the song was saying—its theme. Will you discuss the theme with your partner—what do you think the artists were trying to say with this song? What's its theme?"

The class began to jovially talk to their partners. I went over to Flynn and Jared, who were, as usual, in a debate. Flynn was sure that the song was a lullaby, and Jared was sure it was a good-bye. "The person she is singing to is definitely dying," Jared was saying, to which Flynn shook his head and said, "No way. She is comforting the person." I stepped in to help redirect them. "So guys, it is okay if you have different interpretations of the song, but remember that you should be trying to figure out not only *what is happening* in the song but also what is the artist's *theme or message to us*. You can have different ideas for a theme. Try that work now."

Flynn looked up and said, "Maybe it's about how we can make it through anything if we have people we care about." I nodded, "That's more like it. What about you, Jared, what do you think?"

Jared sighed dramatically. "I guess, I don't know, like, 'Sometimes it's better to lie to people than to tell them the horrible truth'?"

Flynn erupted in disbelief, and the debate continued. It was my turn to sigh now as I convened the class's attention.

Quickly recap a few of the themes you overheard.

"Wow—you just came up with some interesting ideas. I heard Winnie saying that nothing matters if you aren't safe. Veness thought maybe the song was telling people to take care of each other. What I love about the work you are doing here is that each of you has your own take on what the song is really saying, even though you're all talking about the same kinds of things. And I bet you could go into the song and totally back up why you think one interpretation is better than another, am I right?" The class nodded and shrugged.

❖ **Name the teaching point.**

"So today what I want to remind you is that all narrative texts have themes within them, and that when literary critics start to look for those themes, they ask questions like, 'What is this text really about?' or 'What is this text trying to teach me about life?' Then, they sometimes write long to grow their ideas."

TEACHING

Explicitly name and demonstrate the step-by-step strategy you use to determine the theme of a story, doing this with the anchor short story (a familiar one) that will thread through your unit.

"So you read "All Summer in a Day," by Ray Bradbury last week, and I'm thinking that together we can do the same work on that story as we just did on the Taylor Swift song. So now step back and ask yourselves, 'What is Bradbury's story really about? What is it trying to teach me about life?' Eventually you'll be writing essays about your own texts.

"To get at the theme of a story, it can help to first think through what some of the problems or issues are within the text, and then to look for how this problem or issue appears across the whole text." I drew students' attention to a chart that I had created prior to today's session.

How to Write a Thematic Essay

- Collect ideas about the themes in a text.
  - Name a central problem or issue that characters in the story face.
  - Reflect on parts of the story that pertain to this problem.
  - Think to yourself, "What is this story teaching me about this problem, this issue?"
  - Write long about your thinking to grow your ideas, perhaps by asking how different characters relate to that issue.

This interaction, while probably the longest connection in the unit, should not last more than three or four minutes at the maximum. Always, always, keep in mind that minilessons are ten minutes in length, and the most important words are those at the end of the minilesson: "Off you go." People learn to write through writing.

If your students have been taught through the Units of Study curriculum across their middle school years, they have been taught this before. Notice how today's teaching point does not say, "Today I want to teach you" but instead says, "Today I want to remind you . . ." Words should mean something—if you are teaching your class something new, say so. But remember that reminding them to draw on what they learned earlier is also critical.

This unit will go most easily if you have reading workshop going along at pace with your writing workshop—that way you will have read the class story with your students already and they will have had time to read their own texts in reading class and during homework for that class, discussing it with their partners in the context of a reading unit of study. If this is not your situation, as mentioned in the Welcome to the Unit, you will want to be sure to plan at least a week of class time to front-load this unit and allow your students time to read their texts.

"So first we need to name a big problem or issue that the main character (or many of the characters) face in the text—that's not usually going to be subtle! When we read this story together, we all agreed that jealousy is a problem (although there are others).

"We then need to recall how the story relates to jealousy, and what it teaches about that problem. So let's remember the story, thinking about that as we do. . . . You remember that there are kids who live on Venus who have never seen the sun. One girl, Margot, lived on Earth for a number of years and she *does* remember the sun. The sun is supposedly coming out today, for the first time in seven years. The rest of the kids are super jealous of Margot for having seen it already, so they lock her in a closet during the sun's appearance, which is really mean. Then because the sun has shone on them, they realize she was right and so they let her out.

"So now we need to ask, 'What is this story teaching me about this problem, about jealousy?' Hmm. Well the kids are jealous, and they act out, it's like they can't help themselves because of their jealousy. So maybe . . . jealousy can make you mean? That makes sense.

"Do you see how we followed a couple of steps to think about theme?" I gestured to the chart.

Remind students that they can use writing to explore ideas further.

Pointing to the final step listed in the chart, I said, "So once we have an idea about what a theme might be in the text—'jealousy can make you mean'—it helps to do some writing, since that is one of the best ways to help ideas grow. Writing gives a person focused time to explore ideas." I opened up my notebook and said, "You know a lot about writing long. Notice again how I use writing to grow ideas, to push thinking. I'm going to name the theme and then I have to think, 'How do I say more about this?' There are a bunch of ways to think through a theme—maybe I'll think about how the theme relates to the different characters, so that'll be how jealousy makes different characters mean, or maybe just the effects of jealousy on different characters."

> One theme emerging in the text is that jealousy can make you mean. Because the kids are jealous of Margot, they keep her away from the sun, they are mean to her. So jealousy hurts Margot, the victim. But I think it also hurts the children who are acting jealous, too. They feel bad at the end of the story. They are not proud of themselves. This is significant because it shows that jealousy is harmful to everyone.

Debrief, highlighting the concrete steps you took to write about a story's theme.

"I hope you notice that what we did first was to name and reflect on a problem in the story—jealousy—and then we thought a bit about what the story might be teaching us about that problem. After that I started writing long about this idea."

You might be tempted to do more question and answer with your students rather than sharing so much of your own thinking. We hope you'll resist this temptation! While it sometimes seems that students will be more engaged if they are being called upon to answer questions, this often ends up turning your teaching into a guessing game that eats up time. We suggest you try this and see how it works. This method of instruction is crucial because ultimately we are saving time for kids to engage in real discussions later as they write and reread.

When writing within a minilesson, you need to decide whether you actually want to write with a marker on chart paper or to find another means to do so. Writing on chart paper is generally slow and, if your text is more than two lines long, it may not be not worth the time it takes. If you have a Smart Board or document camera and can write at top speed on notebook paper while your writing is being enlarged, then do that. Otherwise you might scrawl on your notebook and voice the words as you zip through them.

ACTIVE ENGAGEMENT

Channel students to try the work of interpretation on another possible theme.

"So now you are going to give this work a go, on the same story. You might be thinking, 'But we already found the theme for that story!' But the thing about themes is that there is never just one theme, one right answer to what a story is really about. The best stories are like life—complicated and rich with meaning.

"Today, when you go off to work on your own stories and novels, you will not just find one theme in your texts, but many possible themes. So let's try that on 'All Summer in a Day' now. Work with your partner." I gestured to the first step on the chart. "What other central problems or issues do you see in this text? As you review parts of the story related to the issue or problem that comes to mind, think, 'What is the story teaching us about this problem?'"

Shirley and Chris began talking instantly. I moved over to them. Chris was pointing to the story, saying, "I think a big problem in this story is the adults—like, where are they?"

Shirley nodded, "Yeah why aren't they stopping the kids from, like, torturing each other?"

I intervened, "Nice work finding another problem—what's your next step?"

Shirley shrugged. I pointed to the next two items on the chart. She smiled. "Ohhhh! What parts of the story go with this and what is the story teaching?"

I moved on, voicing over to the whole class, "Don't forget to let the chart guide you."

After another minute, I brought the class together. "Wow. I have to say I can really see how much you learned in sixth and seventh grade about thinking through themes in texts. Shirley and Chris said that this story is teaching us that left alone, kids will be cruel to each other. That kids need adults. And Glen and Lucas talked about how the story teaches that being different is difficult. Really nice work. Of course, if you were working on this story on your own, you would go off and write long about your ideas, trying to grow and to complicate them."

Notice that when you are referring back to steps in a strategy, it is helpful to repeat the exact words you used earlier for those steps so that students see that you are not teaching them something new, you are simply threading that prior instruction into their work. Eventually, of course, once students have internalized these steps so they are second nature to them, you can talk about them using lots of different language to describe what you hope students are doing, but you just taught kids to follow these steps— for now, it is important to keep your language consistent.

Moving on is important. Think of yourself as listening, nudging, and then leaving. And if you find yourself needing to say the same nudge to several sets of partners, then you know to say this as a quick voiceover to the entire class.

.LINK

Encourage your students to set goals for their work that day.

"So today your work will be to think and write about the themes coming up in your *own* stories. You've all selected a text that you have read completely by now. Some of you may need to do some more rereading and annotating to get your thoughts clear. I've shown you one process for thinking about theme—start with the problems of a text, recall the parts of the story that relate to this problem, think about what the text is teaching about this problem, and then write long to grow your ideas. But some of you may have other ways to get yourselves thinking and writing about the themes in your text. Once you have a theme in mind, get started and plan to write at least a page and a half or two pages today. This will probably be one entry about the text—it is about reading but do it in your writer's notebook—but it could be two shorter entries.

"Right now, get started. If some of you have trouble getting started, gather around me and I'll give you a leg up."

Ambitious Teaching that Gets Students off to a Productive Start

AT THE END OF YOUR MINILESSON, you set things up so that you will first support those students who are not confident that they can get started without support. A student who is new to your school, or one who has not had the full course of work outlined in this middle school series, may not have had enough experience reflecting on the themes of a text to feel confident working independently at the start of today's work time. You could suggest those students look for a minute at another text they know well, guiding them to work in temporary partnerships (with others in this hastily convened group) through a simple version of this work, done with that text. In this way, the small-group work becomes a second, very quick minilesson, only instead of you doing the work in front of the class, you give the students directions to proceed, step by step, to do the work themselves.

After they have done the work very quickly with a text they know well, you could then ask them to look at their own texts, and instead of suggesting they stare at the pages until the idea for a theme comes to mind, you could point out that the reason themes are called "universal themes" is that many of them repeat across stories. Suggest they take whatever theme they found in the text just studied and see if, perhaps, a variation of that same theme might be embedded in the novel they are reading. Then again, they could take one of a handful of common themes and try any one of those on for size.

You will also find students who have trouble accessing all they know from prior years of instruction. Take heart—your students' shrugging of shoulders is not uncommon, and just a few tiny visual clues can usually bring all they know flooding back. People benefit from warm-ups, visual cues and quick reminders that help them remember the details of something long past. And for eighth-graders, a year is a long time indeed! So if you have some kind of artifact for them to study—a photo of a chart from last year's teaching, or your students' old reading notebooks—you can ask students to look this over so that it jogs their memory. Channel them to have a quick discussion about how the work they did last year can help them with the work of today, of this unit.

Perhaps foremost among other reminders will be charts about essay structures. You are asking students to write entries, not essays, but they will be proposing a theme and writing about the evidence in a text that supports that theme—and the easiest way to do this writing is within an essay structure. So watch for whether they draw upon what they know about essays to write, and if they don't, ask about that.

As you talk with students about the novel they are studying and their ideas about that novel, watch closely for evidence of whether the student is actually able to read that book. Many eighth-graders, when asked whether they feel like they can do this high level of work in a book that is significantly too hard for them to read, will admit honestly that they cannot. To assess this, you might try to deliberately set students up to read passages to you that support one theme or another, just so that you have windows into whether this is a text that the students can read easily. If the student doesn't read the text with fluency, including the intonation that suggests the student is comprehending the text, don't waste a moment before getting the student to switch to an easier book. Offer students the chance to return to a familiar text that is a far better fit, and create an action plan with your students so that they "catch up" on the work of the unit so far. Dick Allington, Penny Kittle, Peter Johnston, among others, join TCRWP staff in making the rather obvious case that for students to be successful as readers and as writers about reading, they need to be able to read the books they are holding. If you see that many of your students are unable to think at all about the themes in a text, or if their close reading gives them no new insights into those themes, then you might check in on the match between their reading abilities and the level of book they are holding.

Finally, be sure that you continue to convey that you expect students to produce *at least* a page and a half today, and that most are writing two or more pages. If your students have not had prior writing instruction or for some other reason these expectations seem ambitious, keep that to yourself. Act like these suggestions for volume are *not* over the top—and believe this as well. In fifth grade, most students were

(continues)

"Class, let me get your attention for a second. I was working with Terrell, and he remembered some of the techniques he used last year when trying to write long about an idea, techniques that he thought would help you all. Terrell tried to use the thought prompts most of you have learned in the past few years to help grow his thinking. Terrell? Will you share the thought prompts you remembered?"

Terrell spoke shyly, "Um, yeah. I used like 'Maybe . . .' and 'The reason for this is . . .' I think there are others too but I didn't use them."

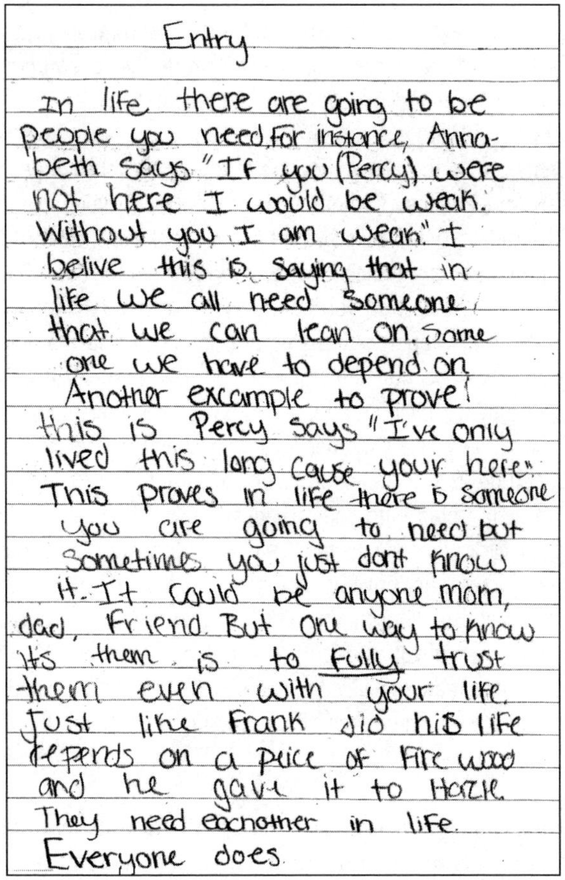

"I bet we could come up with a good list here today of some thought prompts that might help push your thinking. Take a second and talk to the person next to you— what prompts do you remember using in the past?"

Within seconds, the class had called out some ideas, and as they got back to work I jotted their ideas into some sequential order, producing a new chart.

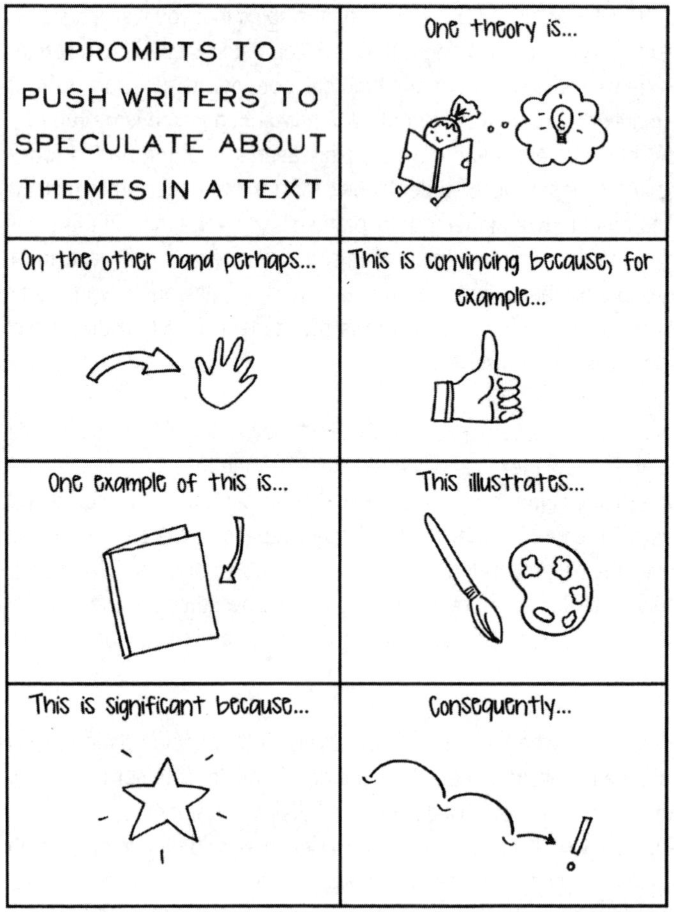

Entry

In life there are going to be people you need. For instance, Anna-beth says "If you (Percy) were not here I would be weak. Without you I am weak" I belive this is saying that in life we all need someone that we can lean on. Some one we have to depend on. Another excample to prove this is Percy says "I've only lived this long cause your here." This proves in life there is someone you are going to need but sometimes you just dont know it. It could be anyone mom, dad, Friend. But one way to know it's them is to Fully trust them even with your life. Just like Frank did his life depends on a piece of Fire wood and he gave it to Hazle. They need eachother in life. Everyone does.

FIG. 1–1   Lara uses the thought prompts "For instance" and "Another example."

PROMPTS TO PUSH WRITERS TO SPECULATE ABOUT THEMES IN A TEXT

One theory is...

On the other hand perhaps...

This is convincing because, for example...

One example of this is...

This illustrates...

This is significant because...

Consequently...

writing a page and a half a day! You'd be surprised how much power your expectations have over the quantity and quality of work that your students do—so ramp them up. Because you absolutely will need to pay attention to volume, call out voiceovers often, such as "Your hand should be flying over the paper," and "You've been writing twenty minutes by now, you should be well into your second page . . ." Say this even if you have to role-play your way into having this sort of confidence. You'll be amazed how much of a difference your ambitious teaching makes.

Writing about Themes of Personal Significance

Explain to writers that although they are engaged in academic writing, it is still imperative that they write from a personal place and with voice.

"Writers, as you are probably seeing, the work of this unit is going to be pretty academic. It's going to be the kind of writing you will do in high school and college, and the kind of writing that you will do when you are communicating with other scholars in the field. When you write academic texts, it can sometimes feel as if you leave your interests, your self, at the door. In fact, many teachers will teach you to never use the word *I* in your essays. How many of you have heard that before?" Hands shot up around the classroom.

I nodded. "Well, that advice is debatable—we'll talk more about it—but yes, literary essays tend to be more about your head than your heart. But literary critics care—and care deeply—about the ideas and themes in their essays. Usually that caring comes not only from the text but also from a personal place. Donald Murray, a Pulitzer prize–winning writer, often said to his students, 'Write about ideas that strike an echoing chord in your own being.'"

Demonstrate that literary critics explore themes that matter to them, then urge students to do the same.

"Before you get too committed to one of the themes you addressed so far in your entries, it's a good idea to step back and reflect on which of those themes resonates for you, and to keep searching until you find a theme that does. Think of a theme you have written about today and ask yourself whether that theme matters to you. Because here is the thing—if you aren't connected to your work, your readers won't be either. For example, think about the class text and the class theme for a moment. If you were considering writing a literary essay on the theme that jealousy can make people selfish or blind to others, you'd want to first think whether that has been true in your own life.

"For me, I was in a play once in school and I did really well—it was the first time I really succeeded at anything. I was so happy. But then my best friend seemed to give these little digs all night: telling me how the director was saying how brilliant my co-stars were, for example. Her tone of voice was really weird and condescending.

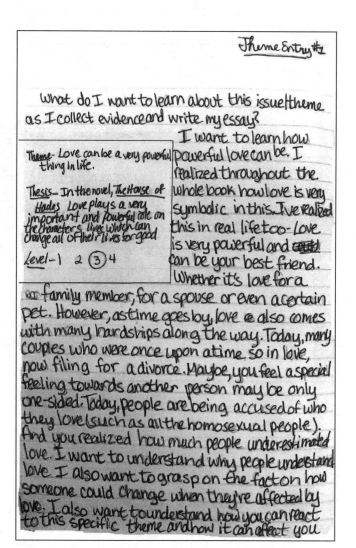

FIG. 1–2 Joy explores the theme of "love" in *The House of Hades*.

"When I think about my experience with this issue, I can push myself by asking, 'What do *I* want to learn about this theme?' And I think one thing I want to think about is why other people are unhappy when things are going well for a person. What allows that kind of jealousy to take hold?

"Now I know today you were exploring themes other than this one. But will you talk with your partner about whatever themes you were exploring today, thinking together about whether your life experiences draw you to that theme. What do you want to learn from exploring the story's message? Turn and talk."

I moved among the tables where students sat, coaching them to nudge each other to get started by saying things like, "Have you ever seen this idea work in your life?" and "Why might this theme matter to you?"

Soon I brought the class together and asked Flynn to share his thinking. He said, "Well I was writing about kindness and how hard it is to be kind sometimes. And, well, like I guess that can be hard for me too. Like I was kind of a jerk to someone yesterday and now I am thinking that I could have been kinder."

I interrupted. "Okay, so what do you want to find out about kindness from this study you are about to begin?"

"I guess I want to know what to do to, like, overcome the parts of you that are not kind. I want to know how not to be mean, and I guess why that is so tough sometimes."

I nodded, and said to all the students, "So tonight for homework, keep working on this very smart work you started today."

EXPLORING THEMES

"Tonight, write one and a half or two pages in your notebook. You could write another theme entry or two, or you could dig deeper into a theme entry you already wrote, exploring how that theme plays out in more parts of the text. The choice is yours, but make sure your writing is at least a page and a half, and that you remember to follow similar steps as we did today. Also, please email your entry to your partner so that the two of you read each other's work before class tomorrow."

Reading Closely to Develop Themes

IN THIS SESSION, you'll teach students that academic writers look closely at a text to further develop their understanding of the text's themes, and then use writing to discover what the whole text is saying about those ideas.

GETTING READY

✔ "How to Write a Thematic Essay" anchor chart, with new bullet point added (see Teaching)

✔ Chart paper and markers (see Teaching)

✔ Your own copy as well as students' copies of the anchor text "All Summer in a Day" (see Teaching and Active Engagement)

✔ Your own writer's notebook (see Teaching)

✔ "Prompts to Push Writers to Speculate about Themes in a Text" chart, from Session 1 (see Teaching and Active Engagement)

✔ Texts students are analyzing for their own writing (see Link)

✔ Students' writer's notebooks (see Link and Share)

COMMON CORE STATE STANDARDS: W.8.1.c, W.8.2.d, W.8.4, W.8.6, W.8.9.a, RL.8.1, RL.8.2, RL.8.3, RL.8.4, SL.8.1, L.8.1, L8.2, L.8.3

YOUR STUDENTS will come to this session having written several entries in which they explore possible themes that they have found threading through the novels (or short stories) they are studying in this unit. You'll support them in collecting more entries today and this evening, and this time your teaching will ask them to make sure that the themes they imagine are actually embedded in the text.

There is for all of us a moment in our lives when we want something very badly and are on the hunt. Perhaps it is a new job, or a house, or even a relationship. When this happens, we scour the world for the thing we desire, and often, we pounce on the first possibility that comes our way, scared that it will be the only opportunity we have to see our dreams come true. We take the first job offer, buy the first house, get into the first relationship available to us. The problem with this mentality, of course, is that the first opportunity may not always be the best one. While we cannot see into the future, it is often a good idea to wait a bit and see what our options are, holding out a little for that perfect situation that might bring us true happiness.

This human truth holds true in writing as well. By now, your students have written a handful of entries exploring themes in their texts, and will, through that writing, presumably have explored three or four themes. Some of those themes may sound quite lovely and profound—and indeed, they may be. But they also may not be the best possible theme for that particular story—it will be important to teach your students to hold out a bit, to do a bit more searching for that perfect fit.

In this session, you'll remind your students that literary critics use close reading to refine and develop their understanding of the themes they find in texts. Students profit from doing some freewriting about those themes. When people do this sort of writing, it can provide them with material and insights that are foundational for the essays they eventually produce.

This is the foundational work—the holding out and digging deeper for the perfect job, house, or relationship. This is you, giving your students chances to hold out and dig deep for their personal bests, to find a claim that will be at the heart of their essays.

Reading Closely to Develop Themes

CONNECTION

Rally students to reread, rethink, and revise their understandings of the themes in their texts. Do this in part by explaining that one of your life themes has played out differently at different moments in your life.

"Writers, you are off to an intense start in this work of learning to write first-class literary essays. You are all fired up to keep writing and writing, I know, but I need to rein you in a little now, and remind you that when you have just gotten yourself started on a writing project, that's always a good time to pause just a bit, and to rethink your direction.

"For example, if you rethink the theme you've begun to follow, and revisit your text with that theme in mind, you'll no doubt see things you didn't see the first time. Among other things, you'll find that the one theme you were tracking may actually change as the text unrolls.

"Themes evolve, they change, not just across a text—they also change across a life. When I was planning this lesson for you, I started thinking about how I have themes in my life and how the themes in my life evolve over time. Like I have this theme of feeling like I don't fit in. When I look at just one part of my life, I can see things about not fitting in that are different from when I look at another part of my life. By looking closely at certain parts of my life where fitting in was a big deal, I can see so much more than when I just think in general about that issue in my life.

"For example, I can see that when I was younger I just plain felt like I didn't fit—I was the new kid a lot, I was different than other kids, I was shy. Then, when I was a teenager, I wanted so badly to fit in and I tried really hard. So it was like I was fitting in, I had friends and stuff, but inside I felt apart and a little lonely, like I had this secret self. And then in college, I found that by learning to be myself, the right people would fit with me, that I didn't have to do anything but be me (and have a thick skin). When I look more closely at certain parts of my experience, I see that really what I have learned about fitting in is that while not fitting in is painful, it helps you to define who you are. That in some ways, the pain of not fitting in can be the best thing in the world.

"In a previous session you collected some entries in which you thought about the different themes in a text and wrote long about them. But in the stories you read, as in life, themes come alive in the smaller, key moments of the text. If you want to understand a theme, you need to look a little closer."

◆ COACHING

Again, this minilesson tries to recruit students' motivation for the work you are asking them to do. You can't teach them how to revise their thinking about themes without first at least trying to sell them on the idea of revising their thinking.

To build even more excitement and interest around the idea of your life themes, you could bring in photos of yourself at these different stages of your life. This is a great opportunity to quickly show students a side of yourself they may not always see.

Name the teaching point.

"Today I am going to teach you that literary essayists dig deep into the texts they are writing about, reading critical scenes closely to look for nuance and detail, and then they use writing to say what they think the text is really saying. This is what's entailed in writing about a theme—reading closely to see how your thinking about the theme might evolve."

TEACHING

Tell students that literary essayists reread the text with theme in hand, noting critical scenes in which the theme is especially in evidence, and revising or adding to their thinking about the theme as they go.

"So previously, you went through several steps to look for themes in your texts. You found a problem or issue that was explored in your texts, you reflected on parts of your texts that pertained to the issue, you asked yourselves what the story aimed to teach about the issue, and then you wrote long to grow your ideas. In 'All Summer in a Day,' I wrote about the idea that jealousy can hurt people.

"But the next step, what I want to teach you today, is that essayists go back to the text to look a little closer and see if there is more there, hiding in the details of certain scenes. To do that, it helps to look for multiple scenes in the story where that issue is present." I turned to the anchor chart and pointed out the next step.

When you retell prior instruction, try to use the same words as before to talk about what students did. You want this work to be in their bones, so returning to it often, saying it almost as if it is a mantra, is a good idea.

How to Write a Thematic Essay

- Collect ideas about the themes in a text.
  - Name a central problem or issue that characters in the story face.
  - Reflect on parts of the story that pertain to this problem.
  - Think to yourself, "What is this story teaching me about this problem, this issue?"
  - Write long about your thinking to grow your ideas, perhaps by asking how different characters relate to that issue.
- **Go back to the text and reread closely to see how the theme works in certain critical scenes.**

"So if I am thinking about how jealousy hurts people in 'All Summer in a Day,' I might list a few scenes that I think are critical scenes for that idea. What do you all think? Which scenes or moments would you call critical scenes for the idea that jealousy hurts people?"

Myah shot her hand up. "Definitely the part where they are talking about Margot remembering the sun."

"Okay," I said, and jotted that scene on a new sheet of chart paper. "What else?" The class was silent, awkward. I smiled and said, "Take a look at the story, pick a scene you think fits." The class looked at their stories quickly. "What do you think?" I asked.

Jonathan piped in, "What about when she is looking out the window remembering the sun?" I wrote that one down too, nodding, and motioning for more from the class.

"And when they put her in the closet! Oh, and the end scene when they remember her!" Claire said with excitement.

Show the class how, by returning to the details of a text, writers' thinking about the theme grows.

"So I think my first idea, that jealousy hurts people, is a good idea, but not great. It's my rough draft idea. And one thing I know, that I emphasize to you, is that by returning to a text and looking at the details, your thinking grows and changes and becomes more interesting. So let's choose a scene . . . Hmm . . . Let's choose this scene where they are deciding to lock Margot up. It's when William, the antagonist in the story, suggests that they should do it . . . I'm going to reread this part—will you help me look for the details that connect to the idea that jealousy hurts people?"

> *The biggest crime of all was that she had come here only five years ago from Earth, and she remembered the sun and the way the sun was and the sky was when she was four in Ohio. And they, they had been on Venus all their lives, and they had been only two years old when last the sun came out and had long since forgotten the color and heat of it and the way it really was. But Margot remembered.*

"Do you notice that the text says that Margot's past on Earth is a *crime*. That word seems especially important. It's like the other children are so jealous, that they see Margot as doing something bad to them, like stealing, or hurting them. And all she is doing is remembering something they have forgotten. She can't help it, she can't help who she is.

"This makes me think that the original idea, that this text is teaching us that 'jealousy hurts people,' is not quite it. I am going to write out some of my thoughts, pushing myself to connect the idea I am having with the details I have pulled from the text." I wrote in my notebook, reading aloud as I went:

> At first I thought the theme was that jealousy hurts people, but I think it is more than that. The kids see Margot's memory of the sun as almost a crime against them, like she is doing this to them.

This is an opportunity for students to practice the work of choosing scenes from a text that fit a certain issue or idea, work they'll have to do independently in short order. Don't be concerned if students suggest a scene you aren't sure will fit. If one student suggestion isn't, in your view, ideal, it won't stop the lesson from moving forward, though you may want to keep these students in mind when you confer later on in the session.

"So now I want to write more about this, but I'm not sure how to keep going." Referring back to the chart from the day before, "Prompts to Push Writers to Speculate about Themes in a Text," I said, "I am going to try out using a prompt like 'Consequently . . .' or 'Maybe . . .' or even 'This is significant because . . .' to keep myself going and see if I have more to say.

> Consequently, their jealousy is so big and so painful that they can't see that Margot is just a little kid who lived on Earth longer. This is significant, because their jealousy makes it so they can't see anything but their own hurt. Maybe that is something the text is teaching us too—that jealousy makes you blind to other people? Or maybe it is that jealousy makes you selfish.

"I like how I went from 'jealousy can hurt people' to 'jealousy can make you selfish and blind to other people.' That feels like a more interesting idea to examine!"

Debrief the steps you took.

"I hope you saw that I took some steps that you could try as well. First, I chose a few scenes that were critical to the idea I was analyzing. Then, I reread one scene closely, thinking about how the theme worked in this one episode. And then, of course, I wrote long about my thinking in hopes that my thinking would go even further."

ACTIVE ENGAGEMENT

Channel students to try the steps you took using another scene in the text.

"So why don't you practice on another part of 'All Summer in a Day' before you work on your own text?" I picked out another critical scene that seemed to fit this idea of jealousy hurting people. It's that last scene, the one where the kids realize what they have done to Margot by locking her in the closet. As I read, think about how the theme is working in this part. After I finish reading, turn and talk to your partner about what you are thinking." I read aloud and the students followed on their copies:

> *"Will it be seven more years?"*
>
> *"Yes. Seven."*
>
> *Then one of them gave a little cry.*
>
> *"Margot!"*
>
> *"What?"*
>
> *"She's still in the closet where we locked her."*
>
> *"Margot."*

Showing students not just how to use a strategy—in this case thought prompts—but when to use it, is vital work. By showing yourself "in trouble" as a writer, and then showing how you get yourself out of trouble using strategies that kids can use too, you help kids to see the relevance of your teaching.

How to Write a Thematic Essay

- Collect ideas about the themes in a text.
  - Name a central problem or issue that characters in the story face.
  - Reflect on parts of the story that pertain to this problem.
  - Think to yourself, "What is this story teaching me about this problem, this issue?"
  - Write long about your thinking to grow your ideas, perhaps by asking how different characters relate to that issue.
- Go back to the text and reread closely to see how the theme works in certain critical scenes.

They stood as if someone had driven them, like so many stakes, into the floor. They looked at each other and looked away. They glanced out at the world that was raining now and raining and raining steadily. They could not meet each other's glances.

I gestured for the students to talk. Antoine and Myah sat in silence. I moved over to them and coached them to get started. "Start with the emotions or traits that the problems might bring out in people. That's a good way to begin. You can ask yourselves, what does jealousy make people feel in this bit?" The two spoke simultaneously, Antoine saying, "They feel bad," while Myah blurted "Guilty." I nodded, urging them to keep going.

Remind the class to use thought prompts to help push their thinking.

After checking in with a few more partnerships, I brought the class together. "You have some ideas, but I think saying more might help you have better ideas. Let's see how using thought prompts can make your thinking more powerful. Antoine, can I work with you for a moment?"

Antoine shrugged. I beamed. "Great. Can you start off with your idea?"

He muttered, "Jealousy makes you feel bad—guilty."

"Yes!" I said. "Great. So now, let's look at this," and I gestured to the "Prompts to Push Writers to Speculate about Themes in a Text" chart. "What if I asked you to take the thought prompt, 'This is significant because . . .' and see where it takes you . . . ?"

Antoine scrunched up his face in thought. "Um . . ." Seeming unsure of where he was going, he repeated, "This is significant because . . . uh . . ."

I coached a bit: "Think about why this matters in the story."

"I guess it's, um, significant because at first you think, like, that the jealousy is like, they're right but then you see that maybe, like, hurting other people doesn't really make them feel better."

I repeated the idea, saying it with great respect, and gave Antoine a high-five. Then I addressed the class, saying, "Antoine took a leap of faith and tried using the thought prompt to say more. That's work you all should do if you get to a place where you feel 'done.'"

Conducting a fishbowl of a coaching session with a student can be very powerful. Notice how we asked Antoine's permission and recruited his cooperation. He is not the student who always has his hand in the air, and his idea is not the best. We chose him deliberately because we know that when the class sees the technique we are teaching move him from having a weak idea to having a stronger idea, we know they will think, "Whoa! I could do that too."

LINK

Set students up for their work by encouraging them to begin choosing which scenes they should reread.

"Get started right now. Take a moment right here and right now to work with your partner to choose some scenes that you think are important to a theme you think you want to analyze—and you and your partner can choose different themes. Don't worry about choosing a whole bunch of scenes—just be sure that you choose two or three scenes that fit with the theme that each of you decide to study."

As students began working with their partners flipping through their books and writer's notebook pages, I coached a few of them toward scenes that seemed like critical ones for their themes, by saying things like, "You might think of a scene where the emotions are really strong around that issue or problem," and, "You could look for scenes where that issue or problem is caused—like where it all begins."

Then I said to the whole class, "Of course, once you are done closely reading one scene, move to another scene that is also related to that theme. Once you are done with one theme, move to another theme. You'll certainly write another two pages of entries today. "I added, "And a heads up—by the time you come into class tomorrow, you'll need to have settled on two possibilities for a claim, a thesis, around which you could write a major literary essay. The work you do today will help you to clarify a theme that you are sure is embedded in the text, and that matters to you. The work you have been doing lately has been powerful—sometimes profoundly thoughtful—and it will all culminate in a major essay fairly soon. Hard work today is really going to pay off." I paused dramatically, and then said cheerfully, "Go team go!"

Planning for Ways to Clarify What Themes Are—and Are Not

AS YOUR STUDENTS GET STARTED, you'll want to circulate quickly, doing all you can to steer them toward rereading and poring over scenes that are critical to the story. If they search for the scenes by starting on page 1 and leafing through the selection, they are apt to grab the first scene that carried the theme they have in mind, and that scene may not actually be critical to the whole text. So encourage them to realize they'll probably choose one scene from the first third of the text, one from the middle, one from the end, so they can be selective. It is usually wise to zoom in on scenes where there is conflict, or where there is illumination, as when a character learns a lesson. You can channel kids to almost think of a story arc for the issue or theme they have in mind, and then to try to locate key moments along that arc.

As students write about the themes they see in texts, it will help you if you are clear about what you really are expecting when you ask them to identify themes. The literature is confusing about this. There are some who suggest that these are themes in literature: loss, fairness, beauty, truth. Others argue strenuously against a word being thought of as a theme. If there is an absolute right or wrong answer to this discussion, we certainly do not want to be the final arbitrators of that, but what we can tell you is that we refer to terms such as "truth" or "loneliness" as issues or motifs and not as themes. We think students' thinking is better when they are encouraged to be more specific and insightful when speaking of themes, so we think of themes as being more like insights. These are the sorts of things we expect students to produce when we ask them for themes:

> Loneliness can tend to show itself when you are with other people.
>
> People are not always what you at first perceive them to be.
>
> If it looks like people have changed, sometimes it is really our perception of them that has changed.
>
> Even characters who are villains have likeable qualities.
>
> Your flaws can lead to great and hopeful changes.

If a student produces, as his or her theme, a term like *friendship*, then it is helpful to ask that student to write about the particular ideas about friendship that the book they are studying suggests. That student may end up writing that oftentimes your friends can hurt you more than your enemies, or that sometimes friendships become like anchors, holding a person down.

When looking for where themes reside, it is often the case that the ending of a book is a place where readers realize themes that have been present in the book all along. Perhaps, in the end, the villain turns out to not be all bad. Chances are good that the author will have planted evidence of that all along, and a close reread of scenes will show that this was always the case and the reader simply missed it. So yes, the ending of the book is a particularly helpful place for readers to see themes—and then those themes can be traced back through the book.

Once students have identified a theme and reread their text, looking for evidence of the theme, you may find they can profit from assisted guidance with this work. The work is absolutely within reach for your students, but you are asking them to do a multistep process, and some won't be able to do this entirely independently yet. Gather these students together and try simply naming the first step and then giving them some time to try that move before you move on to step two. Cheer them on as they work on a step; give them courage to take on more of the work. Above all, try to avoid doing the work for them—hold back that beautiful instinct to say, "What about loss? Do you think the story might be about loss?" Avoid that, because as soon as you have said those words, your student will nod vigorously, learning that if he delays long enough, you will eventually do the work for him, and furthering the belief that really, he probably can't do it independently anyway. Instead, push students to have an idea, and then even if the ideas are not as good as yours would have been, move them on. Keep in mind that if a student suggests a theme that actually does not pay off across the entire book, learning to deal with this is exactly the work they should be doing. Every writer runs into those dead ends!

"Writers, I have one important tip. A famous writer named Richard Price once gave this writing advice. 'The bigger the idea, the smaller you write.' I'm telling you this because many of you are writing about themes that are big lofty ideas. We have themes in play such as, 'You learn more from your enemies than from your friends,' and 'Sometimes the cruelest thing people can do to each other is to tell the truth.' Those are big ideas. You'll remember last year you learned about the ladder of abstraction. If you are going to write about big ideas, remember that your writing needs to also be about concrete things.

"Eudora Welty, a great writer, once wrote a literary essay about E. B. White's book, *Charlotte's Web*. She wrote that the book is about friendship on earth, trust and treachery . . . but in her essay she also included details like these: Wilbur, responsive to the song of the crickets, has long eyelashes, and she described him as subject to feints of embarrassment. She wrote about Charlotte, the spider, saying she is 'about the size of a gumdrop' and that she has eight legs and can wave them in friendly greeting. She added, 'When her friends wake up in the morning she says "Salutations!"—in spite of sometimes having been up all night herself, working.'

"Do you see that Eudora Welty writes with teeny tiny precise detail, bringing her characters to life? More than this, to do so, she actually lifts key words and key details from the book. The long eyelashes, the call, 'Salutations!' . . . those were all E. B. White's intention, and all that Eudora Welty did was to value them enough to bring them into her essay. Do the same. Bring in the detail, especially because you are writing about big ideas.

"Please think about this as you get back to work."

"I'm sorry Manchee!"
"Todd?" he barks, confused and scared and watching me leave him behind. "Todd?"
"Manchee!" I scream. Aaron brings his free hand toward my dog. "MANCHEE!"
"Todd?" And Aaron wrenches his arms and there's a crack and a scream and a cut off yelp that tears my heart in two forever and ever." Todd's feelings towards Viola supersede his bond with Manchee, and Todd couldn't have it both ways so he had to choose what he thought to be morally right. Although Manchee's death is heartbreaking to Todd, Viola means the world to him and at this point, Todd would do anything to save her. After all, life is about choosing what you believe to be morally right and many risks have to be taken in order to overcome obstacles.
    A morally wrong decision could lead to disastrous consequences, but the almighty Todd gets through his toughest decisions by consulting his intuition and thinking about what he believes to be morally right. Todd's mistakes are truly based on pure and innocent feelings. "We are the choices we make" and that, in my eyes, means that Todd truly has a pure soul, truly is warm-hearted, and truly means well. Todd makes the decisions

FIG. 2–1   Rachel's attention to detail supports her big theme.

Revising Your Ideas about Theme

Share with students that they can expect their ideas about the theme of a book to change as they explore the theme further.

"Writers, by now you should have written about six entries exploring the theme in your novel. I know they are all locked into your writer's notebooks so that you can't spread them in front of you, but pretend you can do so. Skim over the entries you've written as if they are spread before you.

"Here is my question. Which comes first, which comes next, which comes next in the timeline of your thinking? And this may have nothing to do with when you wrote them. But which represents the first thought you had about this book, which represents the next, and which, the most recent? I'm going to give you some time to figure that out for your essays."

I let the students work on this, and then I said, "So will you get together with your partner and will you talk about your journey of thinking about this book. Say to your partner, 'At first I thought . . . ,' and then tell about whichever idea seems to you to be first in this progression, and then say, 'But recently I realized . . . ,' and share the idea that seems most recent to you. As you do this, will you be thinking about what your *next* idea in this journey of thought is going to be. Turn and talk."

As the students talked, I moved among them. Then I said, "Writers, can I tell you what Rochelle realized as she was talking? She told her partner about how recently she has been thinking that the novel, *Divergent*, is about how it is important to believe in yourself, but when she tried to talk about it, she realized the idea absolutely isn't working for her. She had been trying and trying to find places in the book that showed her idea—but finally she realized she was actually faking it. That wasn't what the book is about at all.

"I think Rochelle realized, too, that sometimes you all are jumping to say that your theme is a cliché: a bird in the hand is worth two in the bush, love makes the world go 'round . . . Very often, you are better off to use your own words to say the ideas that a book has given you. And in any case, if an idea isn't actually fitting the specifics of the book, change the idea! Be like Rochelle."

COLLECTING ENTRIES ABOUT TEXT THEMES

"So writers, tonight you are going to continue collecting entries about the themes in your texts. As you work, I suggest you go back and forth between previous work and today's—that you spend some time writing about the big ideas—the themes—in your texts, but that you also zoom in on critical scenes in your texts to see what those scenes reveal about the theme. By tomorrow you should have at least two more pages written in your notebook—those pages will be entries like earlier ones and today's, so they may be either many shorter entries or several longer ones. Tomorrow will be our last collecting session before you select a claim to write on, so the more work you do tonight the more choices you will have tomorrow!"

Fine-Tuning Themes by Studying Author's Craft

MANY OF YOU REMEMBER the exhilaration of a time you felt like you really "got" the way in which elements of a story click together to make a statement. What a charge it was to realize that the title, the choice of an opening scene, the characters' names, the repetition of an image—all this and more was done on purpose! Eureka! Perhaps for you, the charge came when you were arguing with passion over *Bridge to Terebithia* or *The Bluest Eye*. Maybe it was a three-in-the-morning epiphany in college when you finally hit on the perfect thesis statement for a paper on *Hamlet*, the claim you had been grasping at for hours.

Chances are, those moments of brilliance came as you pored over details of the texts in question. You dug in, reading and rereading well-loved passages, and suddenly you saw what had been before your eyes all along. It is likely that as you reread, you noticed not just *what* the author was saying in these texts, but *how* the author said it. You mined these texts deeply, sifting through all of the details until bigger and better ideas emerged from your original thinking. You realized that being able to lead others with confidence through your thinking about a story must be the way a tour guide with a flashlight feels—*this* word, *this* metaphor, *this* sentence structure reveals my idea.

This session is about handing your students a flashlight.

Your students will come to this session thinking they have unlocked the secrets of the text they are analyzing. They have spent days generating entries about their ideas about theme, reaching toward a possible claim for their own analytical essays, finding critical scenes in the text to support their thinking. Now you will tell them that the work they have done is a start, not a finish, and they are now ready to reread parts of the story closely, truly looking at the literary choices that the author made. This isn't new work for your students—assuming their seventh-grade teacher taught *Writing About Reading* last year, your students will have had rich experience explaining ways in which authors use craft moves to achieve specific purposes. This unit stands on the shoulders of that one, and specifically, the unit aims to extend the work students have already done in seeing the intersection of theme, structure, and craft.

IN THIS SESSION, you'll teach students that when analyzing a text, literary essayists pay attention to the details of the plot and character development as well as the author's crafting decisions, reflecting on the connection between the author's message and his or her craft.

GETTING READY

✔ Your own copy as well as students' copies of the shared class text "All Summer in a Day" (see Teaching and Active Engagement)

✔ "Literary Devices that Authors Use to Highlight Themes" chart (see Teaching and Active Engagement)

✔ Your own writer's notebook with an entry showing a connection between author's craft and theme (see Teaching and Active Engagement)

✔ "How to Write a Thematic Essay" anchor chart (see Link)

✔ Possible claims for an essay on the shared class text, enlarged for students to see (see Share)

COMMON CORE STATE STANDARDS: W.8.1, W.8.3.d, W.8.4, W.8.5, W.8.9.a, RL.8.1, RL.8.2, RL.8.3, RL.8.4, RL.8.10, SL.8.1, SL.8.2, SL.8.3, SL.8.4, SL.8.6, L.8.1, L.8.2, L.8.3, L.8.5

Today, you will teach your students that if their interpretation of a text holds, they should be able to show that the craft moves the author used can provide additional evidence for the theme readers see in the text. Today, then, is a day for rereading parts of their novels closely, looking with a magnifying glass at the authorial choices, and testing out, mulling over, the extent to which those do and do not support the thinking students are doing about their text. By tomorrow, you will ask your students to have a claim and plan for their essay. This close, careful rereading and rethinking work will support students in developing even stronger themes and evidence.

"Your thinking about a story must be the way a tour guide feels—this word, this metaphor, this sentence structure reveals my idea."

This work will help students weave a stronger connection between an author's message and his or her craft. In a larger sense, this work helps prepare students for the kinds of literary analysis they'll do in high school and college, moving them further from the temptation of simply mining a text for events or quotes that back up an idea and closer to the work of using an author's style, not just his or her plot, to inform thinking about texts.

Fine-Tuning Themes by Studying Author's Craft

CONNECTION

Frame a study of author's craft in a way that your students can immediately understand.

"The other night I was out with some friends, and we got to laughing about how we speak. Like, one of my friends always ends her sentences with a question mark? She uptalks? Like all the time? And then my other friend speaks in these urgent short sentences. Like she really means what she is saying. Really. All the time. The way my friends speak is as much a part of them as the qualities they have or their beliefs. In fact, the *way* they speak shows something central about them—when my friend uptalks it shows how much she wants to connect with others, to get them nodding along. And when my other friend speaks abruptly it shows how passionate she is about life. The way they speak is kind of their style, but it's more than that—the way people speak reflects who they are.

"I bet you have a friend or family member who speaks in a really unique way that shows something central about them. Take a second and with your partner—act out how someone you love speaks."

Students began talking to each other and soon the room was full of laughter as kids imitated their loved ones. I brought them together. "So we know that people in our lives talk a certain way, with a certain intonation, or phrasing, or rhythm. And it's not just *what* these people are saying that helps us understand what they mean; *how* they say it plays a part, too. Authors are the same way—authors 'speak' in ways that highlight their central ideas, their themes, and as essayists we can look to their work, notice these choices, and think about them."

In this connection, we aim to try and make what sometimes feels remote for students—author's craft—more relatable, by linking it to a way of seeing the world that our middle-schoolers will be very familiar with. While the link may not be exact—the way a person speaks is not precisely the same thing as an author's craft—making this connection serves the higher purpose of making the work of analyzing an author's craft feel more accessible.

❖ Name the teaching point.

"Today I want to teach you that when literary essayists are analyzing a text, they pay careful attention to not just the details of the plot, but to the details of the author's craft as well. There is a connection between the author's message and his or her craft. Literary essayists can use this craft analysis to inform their thinking about the text."

TEACHING AND ACTIVE ENGAGEMENT

Teach writers it helps to revisit critical scenes that reveal the theme, noting the craft moves the author has used and reflecting on their purpose.

"So, writers, we spoke previously about how, when preparing to write a literary essay that explores a theme in the text, essayists look for critical scenes that advance their ideas about the text, rereading these scenes closely. But another thing that essayists should examine is the crafting decisions that the author has made. Were there specific literary devices the author used to advance his or her message?

Pulling out my copy of the short story, I continued. "Let's work on this idea I had about jealousy making people selfish and blind to others. Again, I am going to look for a critical scene. I think the scene when the children lock Margot in the closet is crucial, so let's go back there, and this time, as we reread, let's take a close look at the author's craft.

"Okay, so we have our idea (jealousy making people selfish and blind to others), our critical scene (the one where the children lock Margot in the closet), and now, let's look for any literary devices or craft moves that Bradbury uses that might help us see more about our idea. You know some literary devices I am sure, but I jotted a quick list of common ones to remind you."

Literary Devices that Authors Use to Highlight Themes

- Comparisons (metaphors and similes)
- Alliteration
- Repetition
- Descriptive words or sentences
- Personification
- Short and long sentences (sentence variety)

"Writers, listen to this passage, and this time, be on the lookout for the literary devices that Bradbury uses."

> "Oh, but," Margot whispered, her eyes helpless. "But this is the day, the scientists predict, they say, they know, the sun . . ."

> "All a joke!" said the boy, and seized her roughly. "Hey, everyone, let's put her in a closet, before the teacher comes."

> "No," said Margot, falling back.

> They surged about her, caught her up and bore her, protesting, and then pleading, and then crying, back into a tunnel, a room, a closet, where they slammed and locked the door. They stood looking at the door and saw it tremble from her beating and throwing herself against it. They heard her muffled cries. Then, smiling, they turned and went out and back down the tunnel, just as the teacher arrived.

You might alter this list to make sure it encompasses the literary devices in the major texts that have been under study in your classroom. Don't necessarily avoid a device because the class hasn't formally studied it. You can tuck in a bit of explanation; human beings learn language by immersion.

"Quick! Tell your partner one craft move you noticed!"

The students talked no more than thirty seconds, and I said, "I love that you were referring to the literary devices using the academic names for them, and pointing to or citing examples from the text. One thing a lot of you said is that there is a lot of descriptive language here—Margot's 'helpless eyes' or the way she was 'seized, roughly' and the way the students 'surged about her.' I also heard people talking about that long sentence with lots of commas," and I pointed to the line in the passage, "when the students are shoving her down the hallways and into the closet, and Margot is 'protesting, and then pleading, and then crying . . .' So now that we've noticed these moves, what do they show us about our idea that jealousy can make people selfish and blind to others? Think for a moment and give me a thumbs up when you might have an idea."

Use your observations on craft to help you think more deeply about the theme. Enlist the class to help you in this work.

I called the group back together. "I'll start and show you a bit of what I was thinking, and see how it matches your idea. Like you, I first noticed the descriptive language that Bradbury was using. He really wants us to feel how helpless Margot is, so he shows her 'whispering,' and he really wants us to feel how swept up the children get that they 'surge' around her. I even think that long sentence is there to kind of show how swept up the children are, like they are a wave almost, not even thinking about what they are doing . . . Oh but wait. This is good work, but it doesn't really connect to my idea that jealousy can make you selfish or blind to others. Can you turn and talk for a moment—what do these craft moves make you think about this idea? You could always start with a prompt, like 'This makes me realize . . .' or 'This connect to the idea of . . . by . . .'"

The class began to talk. As I listened in to Alec and Raymond I heard Alec say, "Well, I guess it's like, jealousy makes you selfish but also now I'm thinking that this has, like, well it hurts people."

Raymond shrugged, "Yeah it has consequences." I patted them on the back and moved on to Myah and Antoine, who were off task.

"What were you thinking Myah?" I asked pointedly.

Myah giggled. "Oh! Um. That . . . , that, the craft shows the theme really well." Antoine laughed. I asked her to say more. "Yeah. The, um, descriptive language really um, shows that jealousy makes you selfish."

I pulled the class together. "So I want to point something out—Myah and Antoine worked together to say how the craft moves show or advance the theme. They basically said that 'This craft really highlights the theme of the text.' That's great work. Alec and Raymond did something a little different. They used the work they did with craft to add to their thinking of the theme. Both ways of working are great."

Even though I am going to be asking the class to discuss their thinking with their partner, I give them a chance to think before they do. When asking students to think about something challenging—like how craft illustrates a theme—it is helpful if you give the class a moment of silence to get their thoughts in order before asking them to talk or write.

Notice that although Myah and Antoine were off task and were not particularly thoughtful about their work, I still highlighted the strategy they used (with my help). While many students may reach toward thinking more deeply about their themes from their observations of craft, many more will see the craft moves as more evidence for their theme—this is good work that most students will be able to achieve today, and I want to highlight that here.

Show students an entry that they can use as a model for their work.

So before you go off to write today, I just want to show you an entry I wrote last night that does this work. Can you look at it and listen for a few things I do to be sure I both focus on the craft of the text and connect that craft to the theme?"

> In this scene, Bradbury uses descriptive language to show how vulnerable Margot is, and he uses long sentences to show how the children have gotten swept up in their jealousy. **This connects to the idea** that jealousy makes you blind to others, **because** the children cannot see how much they are hurting Margot. The long sentence, "They surged about her, caught her up and bore her, protesting, and then pleading, and then crying, back into a tunnel, a room, a closet, where they slammed and locked the door," shows them almost not knowing what they were doing. They are caught up in their own jealousy. **This makes me realize that** this story shows us that when you get caught up in your own pain, you can hurt other people. Bradbury **uses** descriptive language and long sentences **to illustrate** how out of control the children have become because of their jealousy.

"Can you raise your hand if you noticed me doing something that helped connect the craft of the story to my theme? Okay, put your hand down when I say what you noticed. So first, I used thought prompts, like 'This connects to the idea . . .' and 'This makes me realize.' That helped me to remember that I was using this entry to think more deeply about my universal theme." Hands dropped all over the room, except for one. I called on Aren.

Aren cleared his throat. "You also at the end said, um, what the craft moves like did. You said kind of 'The author uses blank to illustrate blank.'"

LINK

Urge students to make thoughtful choices as they write, today and every day.

I reconvened the class. "Writers, this is some powerful work you've been trying today. You've learned that one way to look more closely at a theme is to examine the authorial decisions that were made in key scenes, thinking about what that might reveal about the theme you are considering.

"This is going to be the last day that we collect entries for themes for our essays, so you will want to use the time wisely. By the end of today I am going to ask you to start writing your claims for your essays. That means you can use any of the strategies we have studied so far to keep yourself working thoughtfully." I added another item to our anchor chart.

It's useful to gear your teaching toward the predictable problems your students will have with the work of a particular session, rather than waiting for the problem to emerge. Here I address one likely stumble that students will make—getting so caught up in describing and thinking about craft that they forget their bigger purpose in doing so. I make sure to tie my theme back into my entry, using familiar thought prompts that they too can use.

This is one method we use for recruiting student attention and intellectual engagement without spending time calling on and responding to individual students during the lesson.

How to Write a Thematic Essay

- Collect ideas about the themes in a text.

  - Name a central problem or issue that characters in the story face.

  - Reflect on parts of the story that pertain to this problem.

  - Think to yourself, "What is this story teaching me about this problem, this issue?"

  - Write long about your thinking to grow your ideas, perhaps by asking how different characters relate to that issue.

- Go back to the text and reread closely to see how the theme works in certain critical scenes.
- **Look for purposeful craft moves the author used and think about how they reveal more about the theme.**

"You'll want to get a lot done today. You should have another two pages in your notebook, at least, by the end of class, so keep going strong today!"

Keeping Momentum High with Your Conferences and Small Groups

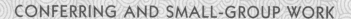

ON THE FIRST DAYS OF THIS UNIT, you may have found that you did more small-group teaching than conferring, trying to get as many students as possible moving in productive directions. Typically, though, you will probably aim to conduct a mix of a few conferences and a few small groups in each day's workshop. Much of your job, as you confer and teach small groups, will be to keep this energy and urgency up while providing specific tips and teaching to support students in their work.

You may decide, today, to pull a group of students to support them in analyzing their craft discoveries. These students might be eagerly diving in, pen in hand, underlining or circling similes and metaphors or repeated phrases, but if they are simply listing the fact that an author used a device in his writing, unaccompanied by any analysis or thinking as proof of their claim, you will want to intervene and support them in this work. Using a few prompts can help these writers say what they mean to say. Try

offering prompts like, "I think the author did this to show . . ." or "The author could have . . . but instead . . . because . . ." These scaffolds can help hoist students up to levels that they are capable of working within, but are not independent with yet.

You might also see a need for some small-group work and conferring today that is angled to help students transfer your teaching from the minilessons and the whole-class shared text to their own texts. Here are a few tips you'll probably find yourself giving in either small groups, conferences, or voiceovers:

◆ Instead of combing the text looking for times an author used literary devices, it usually works to turn to portions of the book that made a deep impression, that were especially potent, and to reread those parts of the text, asking, "What did the author do here that made this passage so powerful?" It probably works to

---

MID-WORKSHOP TEACHING   **Adopting the Voice of a Literary Scholar**

"Writers, hold up for one second. I just noticed Molly rereading her draft, crossing out some phrases and substituting others. I asked her to explain, and listen to what she said.

"Molly said, 'Well, I just thought I could take out the places where I used plain words to describe what an author had done, like when I said the author used repeated sounds. I crossed that out and said the author uses *alliteration*. It just sounds better.'"

Then I added, "I was so excited by Molly's work that she and I started looking all over her draft for places where her words could sound more scholarly. We pretended to be professors in college, lecturing each other about the text. Check out the changes. I'll read lines from Molly's first draft, then she'll read how those same lines go in her new draft."

I read Molly's first draft:

The repeated sounds make it feel like you are in the action of the scene.

And then Molly read:

Collins's use of alliteration plunges the reader into the action of the scene.

"Right now, take the last few sentences you just wrote and you have three minutes to rewrite those sentences to make them more scholarly. Go!" After three minutes, I asked students to show each other what they'd done, and then I said, "As you go forward, see if you can find places where your language can become more scholarly."

---

reread that brief passage a number of times, looking for both the smaller and the larger moves an author made.

◆ Sometimes students will seem very skilled at locating places in the text where the author wrote beautifully, and less able to use the technical language—simile, metaphor, personification, and the like—to name what the author has done. In such an instance, *you* will want to name what you see. Come straight out and tell the student you notice that he or she shies away from the technical domain-specific language. Then you can encourage the student to remember that this is a time for drafting, for messing up, for trying things out—even if it's new or feels difficult.

◆ As you confer, if you sense that these students do, in fact, know that authors make comparisons to things, but can't remember exactly what *metaphor* means,

take a moment and let your students explore the text unencumbered by lists of devices. Have them simply notice things that they think the author did to make his or her writing interesting—phrases or sentences that pop out. As they do, encourage them to look at the list you offered earlier and see if any of the academic language there resonates for them.

As you do this work, help students to understand that words have tone. A story is not just set in winter—winter can be glistening, white, full of promise, or winter can bury everything and everyone, creating a barren landscape. Winter can bring people in before the fire, or make a person wrap her arms around herself and curl into a ball, blowing into her hands, her face buried in her collar. This kind of craft can be another way that writers advance a theme, and students would be wise to draw on this as a source of potential craft-as-evidence.

Writing Claims

Coach your students to begin crafting their claims and essay plans based on their work today.

"Writers, as we end class today, I want to remind you that tomorrow you are going to begin drafting your essays. Before you do that, you need to have a strong claim and a plan for supporting it. Use your partner now to begin thinking about your plan. Quick, you have three minutes to start that work!"

As students talked and worked, I revealed possible claims I'd written for my essay:

Possible Claims for "All Summer in a Day"

Jealousy makes people selfish.

When jealousy and grief get the best of us, everyone suffers.

When you act out of jealousy, you will feel guilty.

It is difficult to watch someone grieve what you never had.

After a few minutes, I said, "Eyes up here," and waited for students' attention. "Remember that your thesis needs to encompass the whole text. I decided that my second idea" (and I circled it on the list of claims), "the idea that if you let jealousy and grief get the better of you, everyone suffers, is everywhere in the story I'm analyzing, so I chose that one."

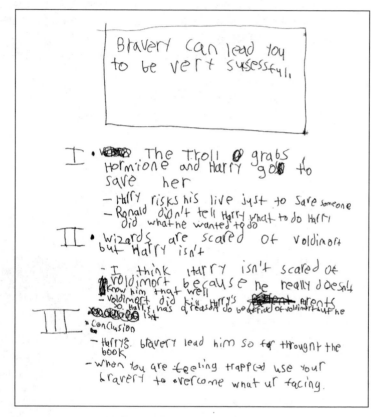

FIG. 3–1 Raymond notes specific instances that support his thesis.

Although I didn't detail this to the students, I think the first idea is a small idea. I could maybe stretch it out into a whole essay but I don't really see why I would—it's almost too easy. I think the same thing is true of the third idea—that you feel guilty. Also this idea just kind of happens at the end so it doesn't really cover the whole story. The last idea also pertains just to that one scene when Margot is looking out the window. So that is why I settled on the second idea.

FINDING AND TESTING A THESIS FOR YOUR ESSAY, AND MAKING A PLAN

"By tomorrow you will need the essay you will write all planned out. To do that you need a claim, a thesis, that applies to most of the story. To test out whether the theme works, you need to imagine the parts of your essay—the topic sentences, and the evidence you think you will use. So come in with the thesis—and the plan for the essay you've settled on, after the work you did today. Make sure you have thought about how you will have two or three body paragraphs that support your thesis, writing the topic sentences for them, and make sure you jot down page numbers where you will find your evidence.

"So for homework tonight, first, be sure that you are ready to write your essay tomorrow, from start to finish. That means you will walk in tomorrow with some kind of outline—boxes and bullets or another form that works for you. If you try more than one, bring in all of the drafts of your plan."

Drafting Essays

IN THIS SESSION, you'll teach students that when getting ready to draft, writers recall what they already know about the genre they are writing in, as well as examine mentor texts in that genre, to make a plan and set goals for their writing.

GETTING READY

✔ Chart paper and marker for creating the chart, "What Makes a Great Essay?" (see Connection and Teaching)

✔ Teacher model essay on "All Summer in a Day" enlarged for students to see, if possible, as well as copies for each student. We use draft portions (as seen throughout the session). (see Teaching and Active Engagement).

✔ "How to Write a Thematic Essay" anchor chart (see Link)

COMMON CORE STATE STANDARDS: W.8.1, W.8.4, W.8.5, W.8.9.a, W.8.10, RL.8.1, RL.8.2, RL.8.3, RL.8.4, SL.8.1, SL.8.2, SL.8.4, L.8.1, L.8.2, L.8.3, L.8.6

MOST OF YOU KNOW the iconic song lyric, "I get by with a little help from my friends." More likely than not, you have a memory of being at a party when this song was played—you may remember how groups of people began singing aloud, grabbing onto nearby friends and raising voices together for the chorus. Even if you don't actually *like* the song, there is something about it—the acknowledgment of the importance of friendship, the admittance that we cannot do it alone, the celebration of those who have helped us—that leads you to hum the bars.

That is the spirit of this session.

Today will be an important day because your students will flash-draft an entire literary essay. Some may not finish it in class, and so they will continue working at home. You should expect this essay to be about three pages in length—and that by the time this unit is completed, students will write essays that are substantially longer than that. This is a tall order, but the good thing is that today, you will provide students with lots of help getting this done. Your teaching today will have two main goals—one, to help your students draft an essay about the theme of a text. Secondly, and most importantly, will be teaching your students to use the "friends" they have in the room. In this case their friends will take the form of mentor essays that will help your students make plans for their work, reminding them of what they already know about essay writing, and helping them set new goals.

If your school has embraced this series, your students will have written thematic essays in sixth grade, and they will have worked on their writing about reading skills (and on their argument writing skills) in seventh. They are not coming to you as blank slates.

By teaching students to use a mentor essay to help them make a plan, remembering what they know and setting new goals, you are placing on your students' shoulders the burden of responsibility to problem solve and to draw upon past teaching. This is important. You don't want to devote weeks to reteaching, and that kind of hand-holding is not what's best for students. Today, your teaching will help your students solve the problems they face, recalling what they've already learned.

Drafting Essays

CONNECTION

◆ COACHING

Point out the importance of being able to write quickly and on demand. Activate your students' prior knowledge about essay writing through discussion.

"Writers, today you will write an essay, so I want to use this minilesson to do some last-minute teaching—not only about essay writing, but also about becoming more independent. As you become an adult, one of the skills you need to develop is that of being able to get yourself started on a writing project and to work more on-demand—doing your own thinking, planning, and writing without support.

"When you are working on a complex project like doing a major piece of writing, it helps to get your mind ready for the work by recalling what you already know how to do. So can you discuss with your partner some of the things that make for a good essay?" The class began to talk, and I circled around like a newspaper reporter, recording on a pad what I heard them say to each other. After seconds, I gathered the class together.

"I am going to list out a couple of things you said make for good essays . . . ." I started a new chart entitled "What Makes a Great Essay?" "First, Winnie and Jonathan said that you need an idea for the essay—a claim. Then Lucas and Glen said that essays have a way they go—an introduction, some body paragraphs, and a conclusion. And Hiram and Mark said that essays always have evidence to support the ideas they put forward. This is a great list."

Pacing is all-important. So when your students were younger and newer to the work of writing essays, you led them step by step through this process. By now, you should not need to do so. But if you find that you have some students who need more help, you can always refer to the sixth-grade book, for example, for help scaffolding.

This chart gets expanded on later in this minilesson.

❖ **Name the teaching point.**

"Today I want to teach you that when essayists get ready to draft, they think about what they already know about essay writing. To do this, they sometimes use other people's essays to help them make a plan, to remind them of what they have learned before, and to set new goals. Then they write, long and strong, finishing their draft in short order."

TEACHING

Show how you read a mentor essay—in this case your draft—analyzing structure and craft and listing what is evident in the mentor essay that can be used to guide future writing.

"Will you take a look at a draft of an essay I started based on our discussion in class about 'All Summer in a Day'? It's a rough draft essay, but I suspect there are some moves that I did in this draft that you could try. Let's read the first paragraph and then stop to name the things that I do here that you could try, too. Then we can read on and do that again for paragraph two." I quickly distributed copies of the essay to students and read aloud the opening paragraph:

> Ray Bradbury's dystopian story, "All Summer in a Day," takes place on Venus — a planet where it rains all of the time. Margot, a recent arrival on Venus, remembers what the other children cannot. She remembers the warmth of the and how beautiful sunshine can Margot is grieving the loss of sun. The other children are j that she even remembers. One le the story suggests is that when people can't get over their own pain, they sometimes end up hurting others.

summarizes the story in a way that fits the claim

names the claim

Ray Bradbury's dystopian story, "All Summer in a Day," takes place on Venus—a planet where it rains all of the time. Margot, a recent arrival on Venus, remembers what the other children cannot. She remembers the warmth of the sun and how beautiful sunshine can be. Margot is grieving the loss of the sun. The other children are jealous that she even remembers. One lesson the story suggests is that when people can't get over their own pain, they sometimes wind up hurting others.

It will help your students to see how you visually annotate the text in a way that would help you as a writer, rather than just relying on them listening and following along. This gives them a model of the level of detail you expect and will highlight how much can be learned from even a single paragraph, perhaps heading off the brief skim-and-underline-at-random work some of your students might be tempted to do. You might enlarge the text and hang it up, or display it on a document camera, projector, or Smart Board. As you annotate this introductory paragraph, explicitly highlight for students the essay-crafting decisions you are noticing, such as naming the author and title, summarizing the story in a way that fits the claim, and finally, naming the claim.

"So one thing I notice is how, right away, I name the author and the title, right there in my introduction, and then I go on to kind of summarize the story in a way that fits the claim. Finally, I name the claim." As I talked, I annotated the essay, underlining parts of the essay and jotting a bit next to what I have underlined.

"So, if I were to take a step back and study my draft, I might be able to add a few more items to our 'What Makes a Great Essay?' chart."

ACTIVE ENGAGEMENT

Give students the opportunity to study and annotate more of the text, looking for essay moves that will help them in their own writing today. Then collect those moves by adding them onto your ongoing chart.

"So now while you are sitting with your partners, take a moment and go through the next part of this essay, annotating what you notice. I'm going to enlarge just the next two paragraphs, but if you want to go ahead and annotate the whole essay on your copy, by all means go ahead!"

You might consider numbering lines or paragraphs before you distribute the text, so that students can easily reference which parts of the essay they are referring to while discussing it with the entire class. This mentor text is my own draft of an essay. I have written it to reflect the teaching I know they have had in the past—and so it is a reasonable goal for them to reach today. As the unit changes, this essay will change too, getting better in front of their eyes.

From the very beginning, the details in the story show the children's pain. They are painfully jealous because Margot has seen the sun and they have not. Bradbury describes how "Margot stood apart from them, from these children who could never remember a time when there wasn't rain and rain and rain. They were all nine years old, and if there had been a day, seven years ago, when the sun came out for an hour and showed its face to the stunned world, they could not recall." This line shows that Margot, it turns out, lived on Earth once, and she has seen the sun. The other children have not, and she makes their world of dreary rain even more painful to them.

Another detail that shows the children's pain is that while they have never seen the sun, they dream of it every night. They dream of gold and yellow and warmth—"but then they always awoke to the tatting drum, the endless shaking down of clear bead necklaces upon the roof, the walk, the gardens, the forests, and their dreams were gone." This shows that clearly the children long for the sun but all they experience is the endless rain. It's not some kind of life-giving rain in this story. It's an awful, heavy rain. In the story it says, "a thousand forests had been crushed under the rain and grown up a thousand times to be crushed again." It seems as if the rain is making the children desperate, which might be why they want to hurt Margot.

I circled around the room listening in, helping students with the academic language they needed to describe the parts of an essay. Lauren and Claire seemed a little stuck, so I provided some coaching. "One way to get started is just to underline and annotate when you see the same stuff that's on the list we created about great essays, like maybe how I use evidence from the text. Then you could try to say a little bit more, like what kind of evidence. Try that now."

Hiram was working alone. His partner, Mark, was staring out of the window. I went over to them. "Hey guys, what's going on?" Both shrugged. Mark said, "I'm done." I looked at his sheet—marked with only two underlines and barely an annotation to be seen.

"Okay," I said. "You know my job is to push you even when you are finished, so bear with me. In the next thirty seconds, I am willing to bet you could find . . . two more things in this essay. You could use Hiram for support if you want. Try it. Two more things. I believe in you." Mark scowled and reluctantly picked up his pencil.

I added a few bullets based on what I heard students talking about to the ongoing "What Makes a Great Essay?" chart.

As I continued coaching into what students did, I reminded them to look for the types of evidence essayists use, particularly quotes from the text, and how those quotes were introduced and then explained. I also reminded students to look for transition phrases and clear connections to the claim.

LINK

Make clear your expectations for the class. Remind students that there are many ways to get to the destination.

"Writers, your work today is to use all that you know to write the best essay you can. But you do not have to do this alone—you have this mentor essay to help you. You also have your writing partner. Don't be afraid to ask for ideas if you get stuck. You also have our charts—you can draw on either one to help you. If you want reminders about how great essays (of any sort) go, rely on this chart," and I gestured toward "What Makes a Great Essay?" "If you want reminders about how to do the specific work of developing a theme-based essay you will want to lean on this chart," and I gestured to "How to Write a Thematic Essay," with the next bullet added.

If you have copies of essays your students wrote previously, you might also distribute those prior writing to their work spots. Actually seeing an example of their own writing is a powerful visual cue for young writers, and helps remind them of what they already know but have forgotten.

How to Write a Thematic Essay

- Collect ideas about the themes in a text.
  - Name a central problem or issue that characters in the story face.
  - Reflect on parts of the story that pertain to this problem.
  - Think to yourself, "What is this story teaching me about this problem, this issue?"
  - Write long about your thinking to grow your ideas, perhaps by asking how different characters relate to that issue.
- Go back to the text and reread closely to see how the theme works in certain critical scenes.
- Look for purposeful craft moves the author used and think about how they reveal more about the theme.
- **Write a claim and a plan for your essay and use a mentor text to begin drafting.**

"Some of you will be ready to write right away; others of you will want to plan for a few minutes or to spend a bit more time studying the draft I just showed you. Choose whatever you need to do to work powerfully as a writer today. Get to work."

Supporting Students' Drafting with Targeted Voiceovers, Conferences, and Small Groups

TODAY, AS STUDENTS DRAFT, you will want to move almost as quickly as your students need to write! As you move around the room, conferring and perhaps conducting some quick table conferences, you'll sense some of the pointers that would be helpful to many students. Don't hesitate to call these out as voiceovers, saying things like:

"Don't forget—the evidence will make your essay come to life. Open up the text and find the exact words you want to use!"

"If you aren't sure how to organize your essay, you could trace how the theme changes across the text, saying 'In the beginning . . . In the middle . . .' Then again, you might consider the reasons or ways that the theme is true."

"Don't forget to indent!"

"Push yourselves as hard as you can today, writers. I know you can do it! Challenge yourselves to get to the bottom of the page, be your own cheerleader—just keep going!"

You may also find it helpful to give yourself the task of spending a few minutes out of your conferring time looking just for what's working. Find those students whose pens are flying down the page, or who are consulting charts to help them, or who are seamlessly blending quotes into their drafts with powerful transitions, and consider publicly praising them through another voiceover, which will hopefully spur other writers to do the same things.

As you move around the room, it will help today (as every day) to carry some carefully selected tools with you. Today it might be especially useful to have a copy of the mentor text you've shown the class, and perhaps a copy of a few different structures for the same essay, to support those students who are trying to draft within structures that might not work so well. You could use a student's work, perhaps pulled from an earlier class period, or it might need to be your essay, in which case you could use these examples.

I. One theme the story suggests is that when people can't get over their own pain, they sometimes wind up hurting others.
   - In the beginning, we see how much pain everyone is in.
   - In the middle, we see how Margot's grief hurts the children.
   - At the end, the children's jealousy hurts Margot.

II. One theme the story suggests is that when people can't get over their own pain, they sometimes wind up hurting others.
   - When Margot can't get over her own grief, this impacts her relationship with the other children, and rubs salt in their wounds.
   - When the other children can't get over their own jealousy, they treat Margot terribly, and end up hurting her.

On the other hand, you might find a few students who are getting less drafting done because they keep returning to their outlines to make small changes. This indecisive small group could be pushed to move faster and make a decision, perhaps by laying out their options in front of them and putting a bit of time pressure on them to make a choice, change what needs changing, and move to drafting right there in the group. You don't want students spending more than a few minutes revising their plans, so coach and nudge them, then celebrate the choice they do make. But despite your own sense of time pressure, don't make the choice for them—they should still feel the burn of trying to solve an intellectual problem—just with you there as a cheerleader and strategy resource.

MID-WORKSHOP TEACHING **Remembering the Power of Evidence**

"Class, pause for one moment. I have got to give Terrell a serious public high-five. He was cruising along in his essay, drafting like crazy, when he stopped and realized he had forgotten to include any real evidence from the text. I mean, he had sort of mentioned a scene here and there, but he hadn't really focused in on specifics in the text and how they showed his theme. So he stopped, went back to the text, and found some evidence. Terrell, what did you add to your piece?"

"Quotes," Terrell said, somewhat unenthusiastically. I responded with even more enthusiasm—"Yes! Quotes! Remember that from your past teaching—that a great way to be sure you have evidence from a text is to quote it. Take a second right now and make sure you have quotes in your drafts, and if you don't, I am sure Terrell would be happy to help you, right Terrell?"

Terrell smiled very slightly. "Sure."

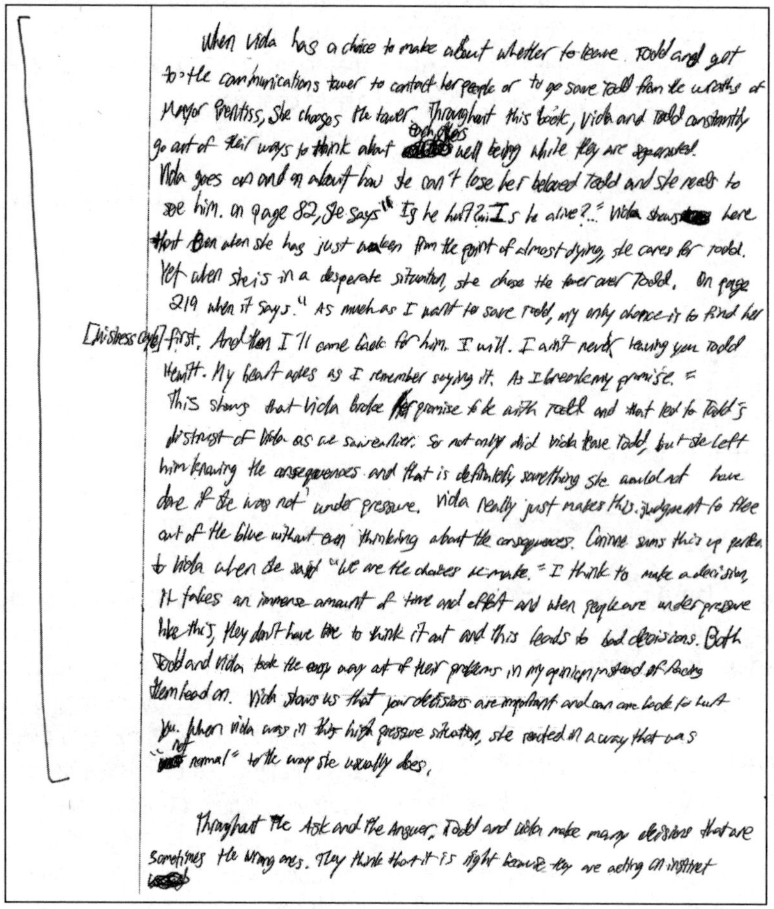

When Viola has a choice to make about whether to leave Todd and get to the communications tower to contact her people or to go save Todd from the wraths of Mayor Prentiss, she chooses the tower. Throughout this book, Viola and Todd constantly go out of their ways to think about each others well being while they are separated. Viola goes on and on about how she can't lose her beloved Todd and she needs to see him. On page 82, she says "Is he hurt? Is he alive?.." Viola shows here that even when she has just awoken from the point of almost dying, she cares for Todd. Yet when she is in a desperate situation, she chose the tower over Todd. On page 219 when it says "As much as I want to save Todd, my only chance is to find her [Mistress Coyle] first. And then I'll come back for him. I will. I ain't never leaving you Todd Hewitt. My heart aches as I remember saying it. As I break my promise." This shows that Viola broke her promise to be with Todd and that led to Todd's distrust of Viola as we saw earlier. So not only did Viola leave Todd, but she left him knowing the consequences and that is definitely something she would not have done if she was not under pressure. Viola really just makes this judgment to flee out of the blue without even thinking about the consequences. Corinne sums this up perfectly to Viola when she says "We are the choices we make." I think to make a decision, it takes an immense amount of time and effort and when people are under pressure like this, they don't have time to think it out and this leads to bad decisions. Both Todd and Viola took the easy way out of their problems in my opinion instead of facing them head on. Viola shows us that your decisions are important and can come back to hurt you. When Viola was in this high pressure situation, she reacted in a way that was "not normal" to the way she usually does.

Throughout The Ask and the Answer, Todd and Viola make many decisions that are sometimes the wrong ones. They think that it is right because they are acting on instinct

FIG. 4–1 Quotes are a source of evidence from the text.

Revising as You Draft

Point out all that your class has learned the last few days. Urge students to reflect on how much they would change about their essays now that they have learned more.

"Right now, will you take stock of what you have learned over the past few days and then look at your essays and think—with help from your partner—is there more I could do to make my essay show all my knowledge about writing literary essays?"

Channel students to plan their homework.

The students talked, and I listened in and coached. Then I said, "So for me, once I have a sense of what I *could* change in my draft, I have to make a decision. Do I just mark up my draft with what revision I could do later, or do I want to spend a little time right now, fixing things. Take a moment and make that decision, either with a partner or by yourself. Then make a quick To-Do list for your homework tonight, right on your draft."

SESSION 4 HOMEWORK

REVISING YOUR ESSAYS

"So tonight, your homework is to work on your essays. Your good first draft is due tomorrow, so pace yourself accordingly. One of your jobs as eighth-graders is to learn how to use your time well. If any of you have any questions about what choice to make, stay after class or see me at lunch to talk it over. I am happy to help."

Finding the Courage to Revise Your Thinking

IN THIS SESSION, you'll teach students that essay writers often have to stop at the end of a draft and ask themselves—are all of my original ideas still true? Is there anything I should change? If so, writers then have the courage to revise their thinking.

GETTING READY

✔ Students' drafts (see Connection and Active Engagement)

✔ Grade 7 Argument Writing Checklist, one copy for each student (see Teaching, Active Engagement, and Homework) ✦

✔ A section of your draft that is not working, enlarged for students to see (see Teaching)

✔ "How to Write a Thematic Essay" anchor chart (see Link) ✦

✔ Students' writer's notebooks (see Share)

A WHOLE HOST OF WRITERS have written about revision in memorable ways. John Updike wrote, "Writing and rewriting are a constant search for what it is one is saying." Raymond Chandler wrote, charmingly, "Throw up into your typewriter every morning. Clean it up every noon." Then of course there is the famous line, "In writing, you must kill all your darlings." There's probably a reason why so much of the advice about revision talks about cutting, cleaning up, even murdering, rather than adding or rearranging. The hardest, but most productive, revision often happens when writers take on the emotional as well as intellectual challenge of holding their ideas up to scrutiny and cutting them, if necessary. This—the cutting and cleaning of ideas—is the kind of work you'll want your students to be doing as they look at a complete or near-complete draft of their essay.

You have likely encountered the problem that this session tackles—when kids think of revision, they are apt to think small, instead of engaging in some large-scale rethinking. If your students have grown up in our units of study, they have been taught, coached, and encouraged for years to see revision as larger than adjusting sentences here and there, to see it as actually reimagining the texts they are writing. Nonetheless, you can probably foresee that your students may doggedly pursue an idea that just doesn't work, forcing evidence into paragraphs awkwardly so they can keep their original plan intact.

In this session, you'll invite your eighth-graders to not only revise their thinking, but also to actively seek out opportunities to do this. This will, of course, lead many of your students to rewrite and reshape their pieces in a variety of ways, leaning on revision strategies they bring from all their prior writing experience. But the heart of this session flows from the last few sessions, as well as from the Common Core Anchor Standard 1 for Writing, which asks students to use "valid reasoning" to support their claims. Part of having valid reasoning is critiquing the reasoning you have, and today you will help your class to see how to do this as writers, thinkers, and students.

COMMON CORE STATE STANDARDS: W.8.1, W.8.5, W.8.9.a, RL.8,1, RL.8.2, RL.8.3, RL.8.4, SL.8.1, L.8.1, L.8.2, L.8.3

Finding the Courage to Revise Your Thinking

CONNECTION

Help students to hold themselves accountable for getting work done.

"Before we go any further today, I know how hard you worked in the previous session. Show your partner your essay! How did writing go for you?"

As students talked, I scooted from partnership to partnership. Winnie and Jonathan flipped through pages of their work. Winnie said, "I didn't finish this paragraph because I wasn't sure what to say, like, what evidence to use, but I wrote everything else, and it's pretty good." Meanwhile, I kept an eye on Antoine and Myah, who were avoiding talking about what they did the night before. I leaned in, asking, "So what happened?"

Myah guiltily met my eye. "Well, I had soccer practice . . ." I frowned, trying to make my look one of confusion. "Aren't you so disappointed? I am! Your essay was due today—completed. Antoine, you ought to use this time to help Myah make a plan for how she'll be able to catch up today and tonight."

Set students up to recognize how and when today's teaching point might help them.

"Writers," I said, getting the class's attention, "I'm glad that almost all of you are coming in with a finished draft. And I'm also glad that many of you talked about this as *a draft*. Today begins some really powerful work because now, once you have a draft on the page, is the time to reread your own writing and to make your best work a lot better."

✤ **Name the teaching point.**

"Today I want to remind you that essayists, like all writers, bring their reading skills to their writing. When a draft is done, writers become readers, rereading the draft to think, 'How does this match my internal checklist for—in this instance— argument essays?' Writers also read asking, 'Can I follow my own thinking? Does it ring true?' And when they find problems, writers have the courage to fix them—even if it means changing some of their original ideas."

◆ COACHING

In middle school, the social energy is what keeps students doing their work. Making time—even two minutes—for checking in with each other on homework is an important way to hold students accountable. When you encounter students who have not done their work, as you inevitably will, be sure that you don't say, "Oh well, talk about the topic anyway," as if it is not a big deal whether they did the work at home or not. Instead, make it seem like a very big issue that work wasn't done that is essential to the whole operation.

TEACHING

Demonstrate how you use the checklist to find trouble in a part of your essay.

"Today, I'm going to suggest you all take the first ten minutes of writing time to become readers, and to use your best reading skills to reread your writing really well, making plans for what you'll do to improve the draft.

"First, take the checklist on argument writing that you already know well—the one from last year—and make absolutely sure this draft illustrates everything that is in that checklist. I want to remind you that you need to become your own coach, and like the best coaches of basketball teams, you need to be sticklers with yourself. You need to be super tough. If you do something that is on the checklist but only do it once or twice, will you check off 'Yes!' and say, 'I'm done!'? No way.

"So watch how I reread a part of my draft for just one item on the seventh-grade checklist—and remind yourself of how to read with high standards. I'm going to reread, looking for how I explained my evidence. On the checklist it says 'I included varied kinds of evidence such as facts, quotations, examples, and definitions. I analyzed or explained the reasons and evidence, showing how they fit with my claim(s) and built my argument.' I'm checking in on a part of my essay I haven't shared with you yet. It comes later on in my draft."

I pulled out the checklist, and scanned my draft, settling on this paragraph:

> Because Margot is so caught up in her own pain, she hurts others. Margot wants to go home even though it costs thousands of dollars. That's a lot of money. The narrator says "it would mean the loss of thousands of dollars to her family." This shows that Margot is not thinking how much money it would cost to go home.

I paused, frowned, and said, "Okay, I'm not sure how well I did this evidence work here. I'm using evidence from the text and I included a direct quotation. So I do have the textual evidence, like the checklist suggests. But did I really explain my evidence and show how it fits with my claim and builds my argument? Let's see, I do say 'This shows,' so I'm kind of trying to explain why I picked that evidence. But something isn't really working. My claim is that when you can't get over your pain you hurt people. But now I'm talking about the money her family might lose . . . it's all about the money and I never really explained why or how that relates to pain or hurting people."

Argument Writing Checklist

	Grade 7	NOT YET	STARTING TO	YES!
	Structure			
Overall	I laid out a well-supported argument and made it clear that this argument is part of a bigger conversation about a topic/text. I acknowledged positions on the topic or text that might disagree with my own position, but I still showed why my position makes sense.	☐	☐	☐
Lead	I interested the reader in my argument and helped them to understand the backstory behind it. I gave the backstory in a way that got the reader ready to see my point.	☐	☐	☐
	I made it clear to readers what my piece will argue and forecasted the parts of my argument.	☐	☐	☐
Transitions	I used transitions to link the parts of my argument. The transitions help the reader follow from part to part and make it clear when I am stating a claim or counterclaim, giving a reason, or offering or analyzing evidence. These transitions include terms such as *as the text states, this means, another reason, some people may say, but, nevertheless,* and *on the other hand.*	☐	☐	☐
Ending	In my conclusion, I reinforced and built on the main point(s) in a way that makes the entire text a cohesive whole. The conclusion may reiterate how the support for my claim outweighed the counterclaim(s), restate the main points, respond to them, or highlight their significance.	☐	☐	☐
Organization	The parts of my piece are arranged purposefully to suit my purpose and to lead readers from one claim or counterclaim, reason, or piece of evidence to another.	☐	☐	☐
	I used topic sentences, transitions, and formatting (where appropriate) to clarify the structure of the piece and to highlight my main points.	☐	☐	☐
	Development			
Elaboration	I included varied kinds of evidence such as facts, quotations, examples, and definitions. I analyzed or explained the reasons and evidence, showing how they fit with my claim(s) and built my argument.	☐	☐	☐
	I consistently incorporated and cited trustworthy sources.	☐	☐	☐
	I wrote about another possible position or positions—a different claim or claims about this subject—and explained why the evidence for my position outweighed the counterclaim(s).	☐	☐	☐
	I worked to make my argument compelling as well as understandable. I brought out why it mattered and why the audience should care about it.	☐	☐	☐

Model the courage it takes to decide that a part of your essay is not working, and demonstrate how you come to that decision.

"So, writers, I could fix this up. I could think about all I know about explaining evidence, making it clearly fit with the claim, and try to make that quote fit better. But . . . as I say this, I'm thinking that if I'm really, truly being tough on myself, really truly reading with high standards . . ." As I trailed off, looking thoughtfully at that part of the essay, I took a thick marker and drew a slash through the entire paragraph.

"Writers—if I'm really trying to make this the best it can be, I have to be willing to ask myself the tough question—does this part still work?—and reflect on the thinking, not just the writing style, before I will be able to fix the confusion. I just don't think that paragraph works—it's evidence, sure, but not the most important evidence to go with my claim, which is why I was having trouble explaining things."

ACTIVE ENGAGEMENT

Set students up to be open to the possibility that their essays could use major revision.

"Your turn. Your challenge is to be willing to look for places where you might make some significant revisions, where your thinking might need to change. Try looking over your draft, and find a place where you might ask yourself some questions—Does my original writing work? Is there anything here that is confusing? Point to that spot when you've found it."

Encourage students to start some revision work right away.

"Alright, you've all got a spot to start with. You could start like I did, looking at one item on the checklist to get your thinking started. Start this work, right here, right now, so you can get a feel for what you need to do today."

As students looked to their drafts, I whispered in—and occasionally voiced over—some coaching to help them. For some students, I reminded them, "Look at the checklist!" Others needed a nudge to get started, or the suggestion "Try looking at a different section of your draft."

After a few minutes, I stopped the class. "I want to share out something I saw Winnie doing—this is another big, bold revision move that I know you've learned to think about before. I saw her draw a circle around a whole paragraph and then an arrow—she was moving the order of her sections because she realized that she had started writing a bit out of order."

This is a moment for your theatrical flair to emerge—you want your students to be almost gasping when you cut this paragraph. You want your students to remember that revision isn't mostly about small, fiddly changes, and you want them inspired to be bold in their own revisions. So grasp the thickest marker you can find, take a dramatic pause, and slash through that paragraph with gusto!

Not all students will point to their most troublesome spot right now, and that is alright. Don't wait for this to happen. Simply having students ask the question of their essay is enough for right now—the most important work will come when students have time to think through this independently.

It often pays off to help kids remember the concrete ways they've learned to revise. For instance, students can physically cut and reorder sections, or tape additions onto their pages. They can also use symbols like arrows or numbers to do larger-scale revisions without physically cutting. This is why we suggest that students draft on only one side of a sheet of paper—it makes much of this work easier.

LINK

Lead students to think about how they can use this new thinking in their work.

"Some of you probably now know you have some spots in your draft that could use some rethinking. Some of you, I know, have holes in your draft that you've avoided writing because it wasn't coming easily—and maybe the problem isn't the writing, but the idea itself. Others of you have things on your agenda today to revise that need to come first, but I do want you to keep this thinking in mind as you're working. Right now, jot down how, specifically, this thinking will affect your work today. Don't forget to use our chart to help you!"

This lesson is not about forcing students to find places that don't work in their writing. Some students may in fact have very sound arguments. But it is a lesson in thinking critically about their writing, and being able to explain their ideas as well as why they are or are not working. We know that even the strongest writers have places in their writing that could be improved, but it can sometimes be a challenge for students to embrace that idea.

How to Write a Thematic Essay

- Collect ideas about the themes in a text.
  - Name a central problem or issue that characters in the story face.
  - Reflect on parts of the story that pertain to this problem.
  - Think to yourself, "What is this story teaching me about this problem, this issue?"
  - Write long about your thinking to grow your ideas, perhaps by asking how different characters relate to that issue.
- Go back to the text and reread closely to see how the theme works in certain critical scenes.
- Look for purposeful craft moves the author used and think about how they reveal more about the theme.
- Write a claim and a plan for your essay and use a mentor text to begin drafting.
- **Search for places where your writing isn't working and do what's necessary to fix it.**

"Okay, you have some big jobs to do today. You've got this—go for it!"

Using Conferences to Help Students Reach Their Goals

As YOUR STUDENTS GET TO WORK, rereading and revising their essays, and before you begin conferring, you will probably want to take two or three minutes to rally their energy and to do some over-the-shoulder research. Rally your writers by talking up the courage and strength it takes to tackle large-scale revisions. As you move among students, say things like, "Today's the day that separates the men from the boys, the pros from the amateurs. Any true pro knows that the heart of writing is rewriting." Notice students annotating their drafts and say, "I love the way you are tackling this with such intensity—your spirit, your power, is so clear just in the way you are approaching this!" Say, "I can see, just the way you are looking between your checklist and your draft that you are a taskmaster to yourself."

By doing this sort of rallying, you give writers time to get started so that you can also do some over-the-shoulder research. You'll be researching not only your students' willingness and strategies for rereading and revision, but also their drafts themselves. You need to identify what the biggest problems are with those drafts so you can address them. You may decide that the use of quotes is a problem—in which case,

by conferring with a writer or two on that, you give yourself the chance to develop pre- and post-examples you can later use as teaching material in small groups or in a mid-workshop teaching.

Because I noticed Joy's draft bursting with voice and rambling on a bit (and this was a problem others had as well), I sat beside her as I do whenever I confer—at eye level, acting more like a colleague at a writer's side than a red-pen teacher from above—and asked, "As you reread, what are you noticing and thinking?"

I asked this, not the more generic, "How's it going?" because always, research that is informed by knowledge will be more intense and intimate.

Joy answered, "Well, I feel like I've worked on my introduction a lot but I'm really not sure what to do with the essay now. I like what I have . . . but it all feels kind of long, and maybe rambling, especially in the beginning!"

(continues)

MID-WORKSHOP TEACHING   **Using Peers as Inspiration**

"Writers, let me stop you for a moment. Something that often helps me when I'm revising is to draw some inspiration from other writers. One kind of inspiration, of course, is a mentor text. But you also have possible inspirations all around you— your peers. So let's take a few minutes to do a super-fast mini-gallery walk. Find a part of your draft that you revised and are really happy with—maybe one you worked on and changed a lot so far today. Mark it with a Post-it® and put it out on your desk."

I gave students just a moment to find and mark a spot, before continuing. "Okay, you have only two minutes to look around your group at the marked spots, to see what kind of inspiration you can draw. Go!" With time ticking away, students hurried to check out what their classmates had done. I held the time to two minutes, which allowed each student to read the marked page of one or two peers.

"Okay, back to work—See? Everyone is working hard today, not just you—bring the energy and inspiration you just got from your friends to your own work!"

Whether people like it or not, love has been around since the dawn of time. Love is warm, loving and is with you everyday. Love is also one of the biggest mysteries in the world and many people embrace love with open arms, ready to find their match. Many people grew up with fairy tales in their minds like a child sings the princess finally finding her prince charming and they mature, hoping to find love like in the stories. However, love can have a dark side and with finding love, it leads to some consequences. Doubts bubble up in you like a fizzy drink waiting to burst—is this person meant to be? Many people feel like the connection between partners have fizzled out and as a result have filed for divorce. And now, there are people who are being discriminated by who they love. Is that why people flee from love? In this specific book, The House of Hades, there are two different scenes that show the different sides of love. But why does love have different sides? And why does love play such an important role in this book and life? In the book, The House of Hades, the people there encounter with love both figuratively and literally. As a result, they realize that love is unexpected and can or cannot be on your side in different situations.

FIG. 5–1 Joy's introduction before revision

Although love is warm, loving and in your heart every day, it is also one of the biggest mysteries in the world. As children people grew up with reading storybooks and fairy tales and later mature hoping to find their Cinderella or their Prince Charming. However, what the storybooks don't tell you is about love's —— dark side and with finding love where are dire consequences. In some occasions there is love that failed between two people and they file for divorce. And now, there are people who are being discriminated on who they love. Is that why people flee from love? In this specific book The House of Hades there are two different scenes that show the different sides of love and and the dangers encounter with it both figuratively and literally. As a result they realize that love is unexpected and can or cannot be on your side in different situations.

FIG. 5–2 Joy's introduction after revision

Although I could see immediately how her assessment matched her piece, I wanted to see what she saw, so I asked, "Show me what you mean." That is a typical move for me in most of my conferences—asking students to assess, then saying, "Can you show me?"

Joy pointed to the first paragraph in her draft and we read it over together. She was right to notice that it seemed to be swamped with voice and elaboration, one line after another, becoming a bit of a ramble.

Of course, my mind leaped to solutions, but I'm schooled enough in conferring to know that taking the time to really research the writer's strategies, intentions, and values matters a lot. So I pressed. "Alright Joy, what have you tried to do to work on this paragraph?"

"Well, I tried cutting some lines, but every one I tried to cut, I thought, no, this one fits my thesis—why should I cut it? There's just so much I want to say!" Joy threw up her hands in playful but real frustration.

I smiled. "Joy, lots of writers resist cutting their own words—killing their darlings, they call it—so it is impressive to me that you resist cutting a lot of your intro. That shows such a respect for your writing and your voice. And I like that even with the voice in your introduction, you still follow the rules—you introduce the topic, the text, and your claim in the first paragraph, but you do it with such spirit.

"But Joy, the same thing that makes you thoughtful about whether to cut lines is why readers will want to read your essay. You *are* thoughtful, and part of being thoughtful is being sure to include only the best, to not waste our readers' time, to be sure we get right to the heart of things as we write. You can still keep your voice *and* show how much you are thinking about your readers."

My goal in that part of the conference was to do what I always try to do—to help Joy feel seen, understood, and to give her feedback that would be memorable to her, that would matter. I went on to help her see how she might choose which lines to cut from her introduction.

"So, Joy, one way you can decide what lines to cut in your writing is to look for repetition. And I don't mean purposeful, thoughtfully crafted repetition. I mean the rambling type. Sometimes when my writing starts to ramble, it's because I am saying the same thing over and over again. I do this because I keep thinking of better ways to say what I mean. But if I am being thoughtful, I can just choose which way is the strongest and cut the rest. Does that help you at all?"

Joy paused, thinking. "Well . . . in this part here I guess I say a lot of the same thing."

I nodded. "So why don't you write-in-the-air, talk out how it might sound if you cut those lines?"

Joy practiced her new introduction, and I nodded, saying "Wow, that sounds way clearer! And it still has your wonderful voice!"

Of course, if you have students who do not have direct quotes in their drafts yet, you will want to address this as well. You might need to research a bit about why they're lacking quotes—because it's very unlikely that they don't know that quotes are needed. They may have been drafting without their texts open in front of them or without using the notebook work they did before drafting, they may be having trouble deciding on appropriate evidence to use, or they may see quotes as an "add-on" task they do during revision, rather than an integral part of the essay. In any case, you will want to coach students to do this work without spending time reteaching the fact that textual evidence is needed.

After a conference like the one I had with Joy, or a small group with some writers who aren't using quotes much at all, you'll have an invaluable resource—before-and-after writing that you can use in small groups with other writers tackling the same challenge. You might look for other kids whose drafts may be rambling or swamped with voice and elaboration, and pull them together to teach them about the smart work that Joy did in solving that very same problem.

Looking Back to Go Forward

Help students to see and celebrate how far they've come since the unit began.

"I have to say, you all have worked really hard on these essays and I am impressed. On days like this, it's often helpful to look back and notice how far you've come. Right now, look back in your notebooks to the very beginning of this unit, when you first started thinking about themes in your stories, then started to study the evidence, and so on. Try to find places where you look back now and think to yourself, 'Wow, I'm *so* much better at this than I used to be!'

"Now write one of those realizations down. It might sound like 'I used to . . . but now I . . .' or 'I used to . . . but I learned how to . . . by . . .' Go ahead."

Students began writing about what they noticed. I crouched beside various students, focusing on supporting what they were observing and coaching them to name even more specifically the areas of growth they found.

Channel students to set goals for homework that build on strengths rather than weaknesses.

"You are celebrating what you accomplished, but another important thing you just did was to remind yourself of what you have been working toward and what you, specifically, are really good at. Tomorrow you'll be focusing on a pretty sophisticated strategy for revision to help you make this essay phenomenal."

BUILDING ON STRENGTHS

"Tonight, you're going to make sure to do three things. First, revise your essays. Take the checklist you've been using home with you—that can be a great resource to help you decide what to work on. Second, spend some time trying to get even better at the parts you've done well already. For example, Kevin noticed that he used to always plop quotes into his paragraphs without really explaining them very well, but now he has gotten better at analyzing the evidence he uses. So maybe tonight he'll go through the rest of his essay and look for other opportunities to do that well. Third, annotate some parts of your writing to point out the strength you named with your partner. Talk with your partner about what you need to do tonight for homework."

Session 6

Clarifying Relationships between Evidence and Ideas

THE COMMON CORE STATE STANDARDS expect that by the end of eighth-grade, students will write argumentative pieces that support their claims with logical reasoning, and that adolescent writers will be able to clarify the relationships between their evidence and their ideas in writing. In this session, you'll dive right into a discussion of what it means to be logical. You will ask your students to find places in their writing in which they might use more logical reasoning to explain the relationship between their ideas and the evidence that supports those ideas. Then you will offer them some sentence frames they could adopt that could scaffold their progress toward thinking and writing more logically.

This session and the next focus on revision, teaching students to build a strong logical bent to their analysis and to consider and refute alternative arguments. Assuming your school has followed the arc of these units, your students have worked in these areas before. When writing research-based argument essays last year, students worked to "bring their readers along" logically, going step by step to lay their thinking down, and they studied logical fallacies. If you are not familiar with this work, you might want to check in with a colleague so that you know the instruction you can lean on and perhaps reteach.

In this session, you'll use your students' prior teaching as a foundation upon which to begin a discussion of logical structure and thought. You will introduce the concept of a syllogism to your class—a sense of "If a, and b, then c," and you will help your class to look for places in their writing where they may not have made their logical thinking clear, or where they may not have been clear in their own minds. Then, you will lean on some structured sentence frames to support their venturing out into these logical lands. These frames will hold dual purpose—first they will help your students to discover places where their logic has slipped, and then they will support the revision work that may need to be done to make their analysis as logical as possible.

This session is the kiddie pool of logical discussions. While you will introduce a simple syllogism—this session does not pretend to cover the bases of what it means to be logical. It is a simple nod, for our students so that they may feel bold enough to step through the door.

IN THIS SESSION, you'll teach students that essayists can use logic, specifically logical sentence frames, to help them clarify the relationship between their evidence and their ideas.

GETTING READY

✔ Chart paper and marker (see Teaching and Active Engagement)

✔ An excerpt from your own draft where your logic and explanation is not clear, enlarged for students to see (see Teaching and Active Engagement)

✔ "Some Ways to Clarify Our Logic" sentence frames chart (see Teaching and Active Engagement)

✔ Students' writer's notebooks (see Link)

✔ "How to Write a Thematic Essay" anchor chart (see Share)

✔ Grade 7 Argument Writing Checklist (see Homework)

COMMON CORE STATE STANDARDS: W.8.1.b,c; W.8.5, W.8.9.a, RL.8.1, RL.8.2, RL.8.3, RL.8.4, SL.8.1, SL.8.3, SL.8.6, L.8.1, L.8.2, L.8.3, L.8.6

Clarifying Relationships between Evidence and Ideas

CONNECTION

Set students up to share and check in on their homework.

"Before we dive into some new work, turn to your partner and quickly show off what you did last night for homework. Make sure you tell your partner exactly what you worked on, and show them specifically what you did to your draft to make it better."

Tell a story of a time that misunderstandings arose from a lack of explanation or clarity.

"So, I was talking to my niece the other day, who is about your age. She was very upset. It turns out that one of her good friends told her he was in love with her. I know. Now, she loves this friend, but not like that, not romantically. It was confusing to her because she looked back now on all of the scenes in their friendship wondering—did I lead him on? Now—I told her I happened to know a room full of experts on this subject, so I'm wondering, can you take a second and discuss quickly—why does this misunderstanding happen so often, where one person thinks there is a romance when the other just sees friendship? Turn and talk."

I moved about the room listening, and then gathered the class. "I wish my niece were here to take part in this discussion—I think she would be both challenged and comforted by what you think. A bunch of you said that a lot of times, it's easy to misinterpret these things. That it's a hard situation to sort out, because in a new friendship you never pause in the middle of a great conversation and say, 'Hey, by the way I don't like you like that. I just like you as a friend.' That would be super weird to do every time you are having a nice time with someone.

"But when you are writing essays—you knew this was coming back to writing—this is exactly what you need to do. You need to be sure and clarify or explain each piece of evidence from the text so that your readers don't get the wrong idea and become hopelessly confused as they read your essays. When revising literary essays, you need to be the kind of person who is always looking out for the possibility of misunderstandings—the kind of writer who is always explaining and clarifying the relationships you are creating between your evidence and your ideas."

◆ COACHING

Using personal anecdotes, especially those that your students can relate to, will help draw them into your teaching. Think of your minilesson connection as analogous to your essay introduction. How will you draw your reader into your writing? How will you help them connect to the important information you are about to share with them? When crafting your connection, you can ask yourself those same questions.

❖ **Name the teaching point.**

"So what I want to teach you today is that when essayists revise their essays, they pause every time that they have introduced some evidence from the text, pushing themselves to explain exactly what that evidence means, and how it relates to the ideas they are discussing. They can make sure they do this well by using a little logic."

TEACHING AND ACTIVE ENGAGEMENT

Explain the very basics of logical thinking, and then channel students to search for what might be missing in your writing.

"So to help you be this kind of writer, I want to give you a quick lesson in logic, because this might help you find places in your essays that need a little clarifying. At its most basic, logic is about drawing a conclusion that no one can really argue against. Here is a classic example of a logical argument." I turned to a fresh sheet of paper and quickly jotted:

1. All humans die.
2. Socrates is a human.
3. Therefore, Socrates will die.

"It's simple, in a way. It's almost like you add two ideas together to make a third idea. But logic gets really sloppy sometimes, especially in matters of the heart. Take my niece and her friend. You can see his attempted logic." I turned back to the chart paper and wrote:

1. She is really nice to me.
2. I like her.
3. Therefore, she likes me.

"But do you see how this doesn't actually work? The first two ideas do not actually add up to the third. We all know that just because someone is nice to you doesn't mean they like you romantically. Today, you are going to be on the lookout for places where you make a lot of assumptions, and where what you mean is not clear or what people would call *logical*.

"Let's see how we can use logic to help make our essays stronger. Here is one part of my essay on 'All Summer in Day.' It's a revision to that paragraph I crossed out a few days ago. I have been working on it since then, but still think it's not as strong as it could be. I'm going to read it and I want you to give it the logic test. First, ask yourselves what I'm trying to argue. Then, look to see if I made that connection clear." I showed the class an enlarged body paragraph I had written earlier, where I made sure to not explain myself clearly, and read it aloud:

Because Margot is so caught up in her own pain, she hurts others. Margot is even partly to blame for the jealousy the children feel. For example, she does not look at them or talk to them during recess. She actually refuses to speak to another kid when he talks to her. And she won't

Notice that today your teaching and your active engagement will be more of a waltz, where you will teach a little, and then your students will try a little, and then you will teach a little, and so on. This structure works for this lesson because if I were to demonstrate all of the work of this lesson, there would be far too much of me standing at the front of the room talking. By alternating bits of teaching with bits of student interaction, I allow myself the chance to teach a sophisticated lesson without losing my students.

I keep returning to this problematic paragraph for two reasons—first, I want to model how much work writers do on one little part of their writing. Secondly, this paragraph can be my slop drawer—full of mistakes and issues—so that the rest of my mentor essay can be emulatable—something my students can learn from. Imagine if my entire mentor essay was full of problems! Not much of a mentor then!

play any of their games. "If they tagged her and ran, she stood blinking after them and did not follow. When the class sang songs about happiness and life and games her lips barely moved." She is really unfriendly here.

"Okay—can you take a moment and help me out—give this the logic test. Start by asking yourself what are the ideas that I need to provide evidence for? It seems like what I am saying is that the children are jealous of Margot, and it is Margot who is partly to blame for this. So one question is, did I choose evidence that can be seen to show that Margot is to blame for the children's jealousy? And the second question is, did I actually spell out the way that the evidence shows that logically? That is, did I use language to spell out the way that the evidence makes that point? If I didn't do this, where is it that I dropped the ball (or you could say, that my logic fell apart)?"

The class began talking. Some students pointed out that I hadn't explained at all how Margot is to blame. Myah said that I didn't make the link between the fact that she is unfriendly and her responsibility for the children's jealousy. I gathered the class together and retold what I had heard.

Use sentence frames to help the logic become clear in your essay, and rally your class to help you decide where the gaps in your writing are.

"Okay, so I know what it is that I am missing—I see that I did not explain myself logically or clearly. So now I still need to do the work of actually explaining myself. Of course I can just start writing if I think I know how to clarify my thinking, but if I get stuck I can also try out some sentence frames—fill-in-the-blank templates—that will kind of force my brain to do the work I need to do. Here are a couple of frames you could use today that match with what you might be trying to do."

If your students struggle to find places that need more clarification, you could voice over a few common places to look. Have students look for any time you use a quote or evidence from the text, as this is a place to check if there is enough explanation. At the end of a body paragraph is another good place to check out the logic.

Some Ways to Clarify Our Logic	
"_____ is _____, because _____."	• (Someone who tells you the truth) **is** (a good friend) **because** (a part of friendship is being honest even when it is difficult).
"If _____ means that _____, then _____ is _____."	• **If** (being deceptive) **means that** (you don't tell someone the truth but instead go behind their back), **then** (she) **is** (deceptive because she says she will keep a secret but then tells the world).
"_____ and _____. Therefore, _____."	• (Being a good cat owner takes responsibility) **and** (I am a good cat owner). **Therefore**, (I am responsible).

"Let me try one of these out on my body paragraph. So instead of saying, 'She is really unfriendly here,' maybe I'll try that third frame:

'____ and _____. Therefore ____.'

"So in this section what I say causes Margot to be partly to blame for the kids' jealousy is, well, that she keeps herself apart from the other children. That's what my evidence says. So I have to ask myself—does it logically make sense to say 'Margot keeps to herself **and** does not interact with the other children. **Therefore** she is partly to blame for their jealousy'? What do you think? Let's have a vote. Talk with your partner for a moment about how you will vote—either yes for this makes total sense, it is totally logical. Or no, there is something off here, it's not logical yet." The class began to talk. After only a few seconds I gathered them back together. "Okay, so who says that yes this makes total sense and is totally logical?"

A few hands went up. "Okay, and how many of you think it is missing something—that it is not quite logical yet?" Most of the class raised their hands. "Okay, so those of you who think this is logical, can you share why?" Flynn shot his hand in the air. "I think it's logical. Because it says that Margot sets herself apart and makes the other kids feel weird around her. So she is partly to blame because she is the one who doesn't get along with anyone."

"Okay, and someone who does not think it is logical yet, can you share why you think it is not logical?"

Myah hesitantly raised her hand. "Okay, well I guess because what you said—the part about her setting herself apart—doesn't really connect to the idea of jealousy. Like, maybe if you were trying to show that she made them mad or made them think she was odd. But you are trying to show her part in the jealousy thing. And I don't see how saying she set herself apart shows that she caused the kids to be jealous of her."

I asked the class to vote again. This time every hand went up for the "it's not logical" side. Even Flynn's. He shrugged, saying, "I missed that the whole thing was about jealousy. Myah's right."

Show how by revising with this work in mind, you make your thinking more logical.

"So we have decided my thinking is not logical quite yet. I am going to need to add a little more evidence or a little more thinking to be sure that I am being crystal clear in my thinking and my logic. For example, I could add some more evidence that shows how Margot contributes to the other kids being jealous, like that she keeps talking about the sun—something the other kids have never seen. Let me see if putting this thinking into my sentence frame helps me do a better job clarifying what I think logically. Okay, now I could write: 'Margot keeps herself apart from the other children **and** she keeps talking about the sun—something the other children have never seen. **Therefore,** she is partly to blame for their jealousy, because she almost flaunts what they want most in their face, while never getting to know them.' What do you think?" The class nodded.

"Yes, I think this is better. So now I am going to need to go back to my original paragraph and be sure I set this up—I've mentioned evidence in this line that isn't in my original paragraph. If I rewrite, it could sound something like this . . ." I showed my original paragraph again, quickly revising it out loud:

> Because Margot is so caught up in her own pain, she hurts others. Margot is even partly to
> blame for the jealousy the children feel. For example, Margot keeps mentioning her experience
> with the sun in front of the other children. She writes poems about the sun, she keeps telling
> stories of what it feels like. Also, Margot does not look at the other children or talk to them
> during recess. She actually refuses to speak to another kid when he talks to her. And she won't

It's often a drag on your lesson's pacing to invite students' comments in the minilesson—it slows down the work and only a few students need to be engaged. However, in this case, I decided that the time spent on voting, hearing two sides, and voting again was well worth it. The voting kept students engaged in seeing whether "their" side would win the vote, and asking for a student response from each side made it likelier that the student speaking would have a strong point to make.

play any of their games. "If they tagged her and ran, she stood blinking after them and did not follow. When the class sang songs about happiness and life and games her lips barely moved." Margot keeps herself apart from the other children **and** she keeps talking about the sun—something the other children have never seen. **Therefore,** she is partly to blame for their jealousy, because she almost flaunts what they want most in their face, while never getting to know them.

Debrief the steps you took to clarify your ideas.

"You see what we did to my piece? First we looked for the places where it felt like I hadn't clarified my thinking—places where my logic slipped. Then we used sentence frames to work on clarifying how my evidence supports the thinking of that section. Finally we went back to see if there was anything I needed to add or revise in that section now that we had clarified my thinking."

LINK

Show students the connection between today's lesson and their ongoing work.

"Writers, today you were able to carefully analyze the logic of my writing and figure out when it needed some improvement. The challenge now is to apply this same critical eye to your own writing. This is work you might set out to do today, in this essay, but it's also something you should be keeping an eye on in all the other essays you'll write this year and for the rest of your life."

Help students make a smart plan for their writing today.

"What I want to push you to do today is to work in a smart way on your writing. You are revising your essays, but you might want to focus on more than just today's lesson. There is the previous session's work, the work you did with the checklist, and everything else you know about revising essays. Take a moment and jot down in your notebook what your work will be—making a little To-Do list for yourself for both class time and homework tonight."

It always helps to keep an eye on how you're framing the links of your minilessons. The content of today's lesson, like many others, is one you'd probably love your students to take up wholeheartedly—and it can feel prudent to insist that students do the work you teach each day, on the day you teach it. But beware of making the lifelong work of clarifying their thinking seem like a day's assignment. Notice how this link works to help students prioritize their work.

Looking for Logical Fallacies

LAST YEAR, your students spent time learning about logical fallacies that can plague argument writing. You may find that this work will be useful today, as well, and it would be helpful for you to refer to the seventh-grade *The Art of Argument: Research-Based Essays* unit as a reference. You might have some students who would benefit from studying how to apply this work to their literary essays. Look for students whose writing contains logical fallacies—in literary essay writing, you might particularly notice students falling into the logical traps of false analogies (William, in "All Summer in a Day" treats Margot cruelly, the way a vicious lion hunts his prey through the jungle), correlation, not causation (William was looking out the window with the other children, and then he leads the kids to lock her in the closet. Clearly, what he saw when looking out the window encouraged William to lock her up), or straw man (William believes that anyone different is totally evil and deserves punishment, which is wrong). To do this work, you might pull a small group of these writers together and briefly remind them of their prior work with logical fallacies by asking them to describe what's wrong with the logic in a few examples. Like your students' seventh-grade teachers may have done, you could provide index cards containing some examples of literary essay writing with logical fallacies—the examples listed earlier in this paragraph would work. Let students discuss which fallacies are represented in the examples you provide, probably with the support of a list of some of the logical fallacies they studied in seventh grade.

Then you might invite your group to reread their own work, looking for those fallacies that they may have used in their own writing and revising to avoid them. Your role in the small group at this point, as in most small groups you conduct, will shift to a coaching role, moving rapidly from student to student offering encouragement and prompts to help them solve the specific problems they are working out.

(continues)

MID-WORKSHOP TEACHING **Defining Your Terms**

"Writers, can I stop all of you? Right now, will you look back at your claim and circle one to three key terms in your claim. For example, Kevin is writing about *The Hunger Games*, and his theme is, 'When trust is broken, relationships start to collapse.' His key words might be *trust* and *collapse*. Right now, will you figure out your key words?" A few seconds later I said, "One of the unusual things about literary essays is that the authors often take the time to do something called 'define your terms.' Now the key words in your claims, like in Rob's claim, aren't words that people really need to look up in a glossary, but here's the thing. Different people mean different things by those terms. Trust may mean something different to different people. So it is often helpful to write, in your essay, 'By trust, I mean the feeling of safety, that the person you trust is not going to hurt you on purpose.'

"My conference with Glen reminded me of this work. He was trying to explain how a scene from his story fits with the idea of—yes—trust. So he took a line in his essay and just said straight out what he defines the word *trust* to mean. He wrote, 'Trust means knowing that someone has your back.' Once he said that, it was so easy to go on and explain his idea. He wrote, 'If trust means knowing someone has your back, then in the world of the Hunger Games there is no such thing as trust, because everyone is trying to survive and play the game.'

"Defining the terms he was using really helped Glen to explain how a scene was an example of that term or idea. You might, if you are having trouble being really clear in your writing, try defining your terms a bit and see if that helps."

> On page 276 of the novel, Wendy jumps off the ship called The Lucy after escaping from a different ship full of pirates and ultimately avoids a fate that would leave her captured and alone. She jumped off The Lucy in the middle of the ocean and is caught by Peter, who then flew them out. Before this plan was set out, however, Peter shouts to Wendy "Trust Me!" Wendy had known Peter, at that point, less than a day, but for some reason trusted him with her life. Wendy, a generally smart girl, most probably wouldn't have jumped off of a moving ship into freezing water in the middle of nowhere if she thought Peter WASN'T going to catch her. The reason, though, that Wendy flew to a deserted island in the middle of nowhere was that she needed someone to trust. She had nobody left. Peter was the only one who she even thought of at all would help her.

FIG. 6–1 Hannah explores the logic of Wendy's leap off the ship in *Peter and the Sword of Mercy*.

After working with this group, you might survey the room, and your previous observations of student work, to target your small groups and conferences to fit your students' needs. You may see some of your students not trying at all, frozen in place, not able to begin. Many of these students will be kids who have not had many essay-writing units in the past, or who have struggled with essay writing all along. Logical explanations will not be within their grasp just yet, nor will it be what they need, and you will have to offer them a different way to explain and clarify their evidence and to show how it relates back to their ideas. For these students you can draw upon past teaching in these units, which they either have not received or have not internalized. Sixth- and seventh-graders will be accustomed to "unpacking evidence" by writing "this shows that . . ." or "this reveals . . . ," and those lessons can be relevant to eighth-graders as well.

You will want to celebrate effort today. Some students will reach for logical thinking in their essays but will still write with logic that wobbles. Certainly you could push that young person further, but it may be more fruitful to give a high-five and ask the writer to keep working. Consider a young pitcher in a youth league, learning the elusive and sophisticated curveball. The first time this young pitcher attempts a curveball, a good coach will not show disapproval and announce that the young player didn't yet get it. Instead, the coach is apt to say, "Good try. Try it again. This time you may want to try positioning your fingers like this . . ." Teaching students to clarify logically is very much like teaching them to throw a curveball—it is difficult to explain, and they will only make progress with lots of practice and small bits of coaching. In this light, you might find yourself offering tips like:

> "Can the 'Clarifying Logic' chart help you?"
>
> "Sometimes it helps to read the whole section, then step back and study the logic—don't get caught up in just one sentence."
>
> "In the next section when you try this, try quickly annotating in the margins what your logic is, what the flow is. Then write."

Celebrate your students' progress, and encourage them to keep at it. While perhaps ultimately your deepest wish is for your students to be thinking in syllogisms, any student who makes palpable progress toward thinking more logically has taken an important step.

Using Partners Effectively

Point out that being a good partner means coming with questions ready.

"You know, I realized during the last session that being a good writing partner goes two ways—yes, when someone is asking for your help with their writing you should work really hard to help them, but I realized that when you give your writing to someone, it really helps if you have a sense of what you want their help with. Otherwise you are kind of just shoving your piece in front of their face saying, 'Help me.'

"Instead, a good writing partner will come to their partnership with a few questions or trouble spots. Maybe you will say, 'I am wondering about this section, it doesn't seem clear,' or maybe you will say something like, 'I am not sure if my evidence feels strong—can you check for that?' You can always use our chart to help you come up with a question. I've added what we talked about today.

"It may be that your writing partner catches lots more that they can help you with, but when you lead with a sense of what you are worried about, you help your writing partner focus—which is good for everyone."

Channel students to write down three questions they might have about their essays that a writing partner could help with. Then have them work together, using those questions as a starting point.

"So right now could you think about how your essay is going, and could each of you come up with a few questions that could kick off your partner work today? Once you have your questions, choose someone to go first, and get started."

Set up students for their homework tonight—to get as close to a finished draft as they can.

"Tonight might be a big push for you—I am hoping you all will come in the day after tomorrow with a finished draft—a good revised essay. What I expect as always is that tomorrow you show me evidence that you worked hard on your writing for homework. So go ahead now and write your To-Do list down—what you think you can accomplish by tomorrow."

How to Write a Thematic Essay

- Collect ideas about the themes in a text.
  - Name a central problem or issue that characters in the story face.
  - Reflect on parts of the story that pertain to this problem.
  - Think to yourself, "What is this story teaching me about this problem, this issue?"
  - Write long about your thinking to grow your ideas, perhaps by asking how different characters relate to that issue.
- Go back to the text and reread closely to see how the theme works in certain critical scenes.
- Look for purposeful craft moves the author used and think about how they reveal more about the theme.
- Write a claim and a plan for your essay and use a mentor text to begin drafting.
- Search for places where your writing isn't working and do what's necessary to fix it.
- **Logically explain how your evidence supports your thinking about the text.**

CLOSING IN ON A FINISHED DRAFT

"In just a few days you'll have a chance to edit and then celebrate the work you've done with these essays. What do you need to do tonight to set yourself up for this? Do you need to clarify your logic? Have you used transitions to help explain your thinking and help your reader understand when you are shifting from one line of thinking to another? Perhaps you'll take another look at the Argument Writing Checklist, and use that as a guide of sorts, to make your writing stronger. We will talk in the morning about how it went."

Argument Writing Checklist

	Grade 7	NOT YET	STARTING TO	YES!
	Structure			
Overall	I laid out a well-supported argument and made it clear that this argument is part of a bigger conversation about a topic/text. I acknowledged positions on the topic or text that might disagree with my own position, but I still showed why my position makes sense.	☐	☐	☐
Lead	I interested the reader in my argument and helped them to understand the backstory behind it. I gave the backstory in a way that got the reader ready to see my point.	☐	☐	☐
	I made it clear to readers what my piece will argue and forecasted the parts of my argument.	☐	☐	☐
Transitions	I used transitions to link the parts of my argument. The transitions help the reader follow from part to part and make it clear when I am stating a claim or counterclaim, giving a reason, or offering or analyzing evidence. These transitions include terms such as *as the text states, this means, another reason, some people may say, but, nevertheless,* and *on the other hand.*	☐	☐	☐
Ending	In my conclusion, I reinforced and built on the main point(s) in a way that makes the entire text a cohesive whole. The conclusion may reiterate how the support for my claim outweighed the counterclaim(s), restate the main points, respond to them, or highlight their significance.	☐	☐	☐
Organization	The parts of my piece are arranged purposefully to suit my purpose and to lead readers from one claim or counterclaim, reason, or piece of evidence to another.	☐	☐	☐
	I used topic sentences, transitions, and formatting (where appropriate) to clarify the structure of the piece and to highlight my main points.	☐	☐	☐
	Development			
Elaboration	I included varied kinds of evidence such as facts, quotations, examples, and definitions. I analyzed or explained the reasons and evidence, showing how they fit with my claim(s) and built my argument.	☐	☐	☐
	I consistently incorporated and cited trustworthy sources.	☐	☐	☐
	I wrote about another possible position or positions—a different claim or claims about this subject—and explained why the evidence for my position outweighed the counterclaim(s).	☐	☐	☐
	I worked to make my argument compelling as well as understandable. I brought out why it mattered and why the audience should care about it.	☐	☐	☐

Session 7

Counterargument within Literary Essays

I T ONLY TAKES A COUPLE OF MINUTES watching the pundits on a variety of news programs to see that these days we are not listening to each other very closely. All too often the representatives of two sides of an issue instead talk *at* each other, making their argument without much consideration of the points—valid or otherwise—that their opponent asserts. It is, of course, challenging to listen to those that have different ideas from ours. It is natural to want to ignore those other viewpoints, to hold on tight to our original thinking. In this session, you'll remind your students to take on this challenge in their literary essays, teaching them to always be on the lookout for alternative claims and ideas.

The Common Core Standards ask us to teach our middle school students, when arguing a point, to consider the alternative arguments and to incorporate these counterpoints into their writing. As our students are asked to write more and more essays, to debate ideas in their classes, and to grapple with complex ideas, they will need to be able to reflect upon and deal with those who think differently from them. This work goes beyond simply stating that other ideas exist; it is larger in scope than adding a part to your essay that says, "Some people think . . . but I think . . ." This work asks students to also weigh and evaluate those counterpoints, and to argue within their essays how their thinking is sounder than that of their potential opponents. Your students began this work already, of course, when they wrote research-based argument essays in seventh grade, reading mentor texts to study how essayists distinguish and qualify counterclaims from their own. Here you will continue this work, teaching your class how to argue that their interpretations of a text are truly the best, the soundest, the most complete interpretations around.

Of course, in literary essays, the idea of a counterargument is a little different than in, say, a persuasive piece. It will be the rare literary essay that argues a claim so debatable that someone could out and out say, "No, you are wrong. That is *not* a theme in that text." Still, in any text there are moments and ideas that have alternate interpretations—not opposition as much as other possibilities. One writer argues that a character is brave, and someone else argues that while the character is indeed brave, the more accurate trait to

IN THIS SESSION, you'll teach students that essayists look for places where there could be another interpretation or opinion about the text, and they write to try and argue why their interpretation is the best one, by nodding to the alternative argument and then explaining why that one is not as sound.

GETTING READY

✔ An excerpt from the teacher model essay (see Teaching)

✔ Chart paper and markers (see Teaching)

✔ Students' essay drafts (see Active Engagement)

✔ "How to Write a Thematic Essay" anchor chart (see Link)

COMMON CORE STATE STANDARDS: W.8.1.a,c; W.8.5, W.8.9.a, RL.8.1, RL.8.2, RL.8.3, RL.8.4, SL.8.1, SL.8.3, SL.8.4, L.8.1, L.8.2, L.8.3

describe him or her would be generous and bold. One writer puts forth a theme, and argues not just that their theme is valid, but how it may be more significant, more text based, than an alternate theme in the text.

"You will teach your class how to argue that their interpretations of a text are truly the best, the soundest, the most complete interpretations around."

In this session you'll teach students, as they continue revising their thematic essays, to look for places in their writing where there could be an alternative interpretation of a scene or theme. You will teach your class that in these moments it is the job of the literary essayist to bring up those other possibilities, arguing as they do why their interpretation is the better one while also acknowledging the strength of the alternative. To do this you will offer your students a few thought prompts to help them through the tricky waters of evaluating counterarguments, and you will push them to use their partnerships to help them see whether they have done the job.

Counterargument within Literary Essays

CONNECTION

Share a story of a debate you had with a colleague about the class text.

"I had the most interesting lunch period yesterday! There I was, just eating my sandwich with Ms. Maier, talking about 'All Summer in a Day.' You know how teachers are—we just can't stop talking about reading and writing." I winked. "Anyway, I was talking about the ending and how the children all feel guilty about what they did to Margot, and Ms. Maier was all like, 'I don't think they feel guilty at all!' I was kind of shocked because it seemed so obvious to me that they *do* feel guilty. We got into a bit of an argument about it, and I realized that instead of me just saying, 'But I'm right!' I had to do more work proving it. That debate got me thinking—what else might I need to do better in order to support my interpretation? What else in my essay might someone disagree with?"

❖ **Name the teaching point.**

"So today I am going to teach you that essay writers look for places in their essays where there could be another interpretation or opinion about the text, and they write to argue why their interpretation is the best one. They do this by nodding to the alternative argument and then explaining why that interpretation is not as good as their own."

TEACHING

Model how you look for places in your essay where there might be an alternate argument or idea.

"I am going to read a part of my essay, and as I do I am going to think to myself—could there be another way of seeing this? Could someone debate me here? To do that I will pay attention to the ideas I'm asserting, and I will also pay attention to my word choice when describing the themes or characters, thinking about whether someone else might have another idea, or might use another word. After I figure out what that counterargument might be, it'll be important for me to refute that argument in my writing. But let's get started by finding a place in my essay where someone might have an alternate interpretation. So here is one of my body paragraphs." I read the bit aloud:

> By the middle of the story the reader begins to see that the children, in their painful jealousy, hurt Margot with words and with force. First they mock her poetry and her memories, claiming she never did see the sun. Then they shove her. Finally, they lock her in a closet so she won't

Telling this quick story here does a lot of jobs. It engages students, both through the narrative and the hint of conflict. It establishes the purpose behind today's teaching point. But also, and just as importantly, it reminds students of the adult community of readers and writers that they will join one day, and makes membership in this literate community seem both enticing and inevitable.

see the sun. The text even describes the children's hatred toward Margot more explicitly when Bradbury writes, "They hated her pale snow face, her thinness, and her possible future." The other children have never seen the sun, but dream of it every night. The children are jealous that Margot has ever seen the sun and Margot is grieving the loss of it. This shows that everyone in this story is hurting in their own way—Margot because she has lost the sun and the children who have never seen it.

"Okay, so I am stopping here and thinking—could someone debate me on any point I made? Is there an idea that someone might take issue with, a way that I describe the theme or the characters? Hmm . . . I guess someone could maybe say that the children are not jealous? That's an idea that people might disagree with. But no, that doesn't really make sense. I don't think someone would say the kids *aren't* jealous . . . Hmm . . . but maybe someone would say that this short story is not *mostly* about how jealous they are. Someone may be able to argue that this story is really about the children's meanness. I don't agree, but I guess someone could say that really this story is more about how mean the kids are, not how jealous they are."

Offer students thought prompts to help them to speak back to the alternative argument, and model how to do that work in your essay.

"So once I have found a spot where there could be a little debate, it's my job to argue why I am right, or more right, than someone who might debate me. I can use a few thought prompts to help me find the way, prompts like these." I hastily sketched out a few thought prompts on chart paper.

Prompts To Argue Counterpoints in Literary Essays

"While some might argue . . . they forget that in the text it says . . ."

"Some people might interpret this to mean. . . . But clearly . . . because . . ."

"Certainly it could be said . . . While this is a good point . . . it fails to account for . . ."

"Let me see how these thought prompts might help me. I am going to write-in-the-air how I might address someone who is debating me on this idea—someone who thinks that the children are not as jealous as they are mean. I am going to use a thought prompt to help me. I think I'll try that last one. Okay, so I could write, 'Certainly it could be said that the children are more mean than they are jealous. While this is a good point, because the children are definitely mean, it fails to account for . . .' Hmm. Well, I need to think a little bit here about what is missing or wrong in this opposing idea. I've just said that it's a good point—my essay wouldn't be very good if I just left it at that!

"I think . . . well . . . I think what people are missing if they focus on how mean the children are is that their pain, which comes from their jealousy, is what causes them to be mean. I think this is a better idea than just saying 'they are mean,' so I am going to finish my sentence . . . 'while this is a good point, it fails to account for how much pain the children are in. They are not born mean; their pain—their jealousy—has made them mean.'

Part of your work in modeling for your students is acting. You want your kids bursting at the seams to jump in and help you figure out your writing "problem" because that means they are intellectually with you each step of the way. This means your kids have to believe that you are really thinking aloud, even if you've planned ahead meticulously and taught the lesson five times already that day.

If you are concerned about time, or your ability to write quickly yet still legibly in front of your class, feel free to create a chart ahead of time, listing out the counterargument prompts. In cases like these, it's not crucial that your students see you write. It just depends on how "off the cuff" you'd like to seem with your creation of the prompts.

"I am looking at my body paragraph now and I think adding this really helps me sound like I have thought of everything—even what people who have other ideas might say!"

Debrief the steps you took.

"So to make sure you are addressing any alternative arguments, you can do what I did: look for places in your essay where someone might have a different interpretation of the text, then use a thought prompt to help argue back, tightening your essay by being sure to explain why your interpretation is best and what any alternative ideas are missing."

ACTIVE ENGAGEMENT

Channel students to address alternative arguments in their own essays.

"Okay, you and your partner should each pick a spot in your essay—a paragraph or section—that you think maybe someone could see differently. Do that now, and point to it so I know you are ready." I waited again. A few students were taking a longer time to select a section and I said, "For now, just pick a paragraph to practice on, and later you can decide if it's the best one.

"So to practice this we are going to use the partnerships in our room. Instead of imagining what someone might say about your text, you are going to see what someone actually says. Hand your essay to your partner, making sure they know which section to look at. Now, when you read your partner's section your job is to be looking for other possible ideas and arguments—other interpretations—of the text. Just like I looked at the ideas and word choice in a part of my essay, thinking what could someone say differently, you are going to do that for your partner. Try it now . . ."

Students began to read, and conversations began around the room. Some students seemed to struggle and I went to them first, coaching by saying, "Remember you can always be on the lookout for a way they describe the themes or characters, that you think could have an alternate fit, like I did with *jealous* and *mean*."

With this coaching Shirley said tentatively to Chris, "You said that the theme is about making the choice to trust people but someone else could say that it is more about like . . . I don't know . . . how to forgive people maybe."

Direct writers to practice addressing alternative arguments by using thought prompts.

"So writers, now with your partners, try explaining why your thinking is better than the alternative—and if you need to, use one of the thought prompts on the chart."

Kiara and Danielle were working together, brows furrowed. "While some might argue . . . um, that Tess is a hero by following her heart, they forget that in the text . . ." Kiara looked up, confused. I coached, "Danielle, it's your job to try and help your partner if she's stuck. What do you think?"

Just as your students may have done in the seventh-grade argument writing unit, participating in small debates within your class can help them develop counterarguments. Actually working out how to argue a point face to face sometimes spurs thought that might not come when students face only a blank page.

Danielle said, "Uh . . . maybe she could say 'They forget that in the text even Tess realizes that she was wrong to reject her family completely.'"

Gathering the class, I said, "I just want to point out that Danielle really helped Kiara when she was stuck—today when you are working, don't be afraid to ask for help from someone who knows your text."

LINK

Make sure your writers have a plan for how to keep working on their essays.

"So today's lesson is great revision work, but of course you know many ways to revise and should use all you know to make your essays better. Take a second and think through how your work might go today and give me a thumbs up when you have decided and are ready to work. Remember to check our chart to help you—I've added today's lesson."

As thumbs went up I sent writers back to their desks. "If you aren't sure how to begin, you should stay here in the meeting area and we can get started together." A few kids stayed with me, and I coached them to consider their choices as the rest of the class got to work.

How to Write a Thematic Essay

- Collect ideas about the themes in a text.
  - Name a central problem or issue that characters in the story face.
  - Reflect on parts of the story that pertain to this problem.
  - Think to yourself, "What is this story teaching me about this problem, this issue?"
  - Write long about your thinking to grow your ideas, perhaps by asking how different characters relate to that issue.
- Go back to the text and reread closely to see how the theme works in certain critical scenes.
- Look for purposeful craft moves the author used and think about how they reveal more about the theme.
- Write a claim and a plan for your essay and use a mentor text to begin drafting.
- Search for places where your writing isn't working and do what's necessary to fix it.
- Logically explain how your evidence supports your thinking about the text.
- **Add writing that addresses alternative ideas to yours, being sure to show how your thinking is better.**

Pushing students to be better partners to each other is powerful work. Knowing how to find and use a writing partner—and conversely, knowing how to be that writing partner for someone else—is a skill that will live within your students for years to come.

This strategy of asking students to stay in the meeting area if they are having trouble not only starts your workshop off with a targeted and helpful small group, but also encourages your students to take more ownership over their learning. They have to assess whether they need a certain kind of help and then take action to get it. Do keep an eye out for those students who indiscriminately take you up on this opportunity—see if they are more eager to get support or more eager to avoid getting to work.

Grade 8: The Literary Essay

Supporting Strong Writers

ONE WAY YOU CAN STRENGTHEN your conferring is by occasionally taking on a lens for yourself as you study your class, so that you can focus your attention on one group of students, or one concern. One lens you might adopt is looking at the needs of your strongest writers. Today, some teaching that could support these students could include the following teaching points:

◆ Some of your students may benefit from revising whole sections to thread counterargument throughout the piece, rather than isolating this in one or two places. In seventh grade, your students learned to do this in their argument essays. You could build on this work by teaching students to think more fully through the alternative arguments, so that they can counter the big idea, as well as the specific evidence. You might coach students to sketch out a quick plan for their imagined "alternative" essay, then look for the multiple places where their own actual essay presents a better interpretation.

◆ Some students might profit from studying others' literary essays to see how counterarguments can look in this type of writing. You might decide to use a revised part of your demonstration essay; however, some of your most sophisticated writers could benefit from studying how writers in venues like the *New York Times Book Review* structure their arguments and address possible alternative views. Your students will find that counterargument is a powerful move, and one that literary writers can put to good use in many ways. Some examples can be found at: http://www.nytimes.com/roomfordebate/2010/12/26/the-dark-side-of-young-adult-fiction/pure-escapism-for-young-adult-readers (Google search term "New York Times Pure Escapism for Young Adult Readers") and http://www.nytimes.com/2011/12/04/books/review/legend-by-marie-lu-book-review.html (Google search term "New York Times Legend Marie Lu").

This might be a small-group inquiry—you could start the conversation, providing students with a mentor essay and inviting them to talk and record their observations on a large piece of paper or a shared document online, and then

MID-WORKSHOP TEACHING
When the Alternative Arguments Are Better Than Yours

"Writers, let me pause you for just a moment. I have got to share what Rachel just did as a writer. She was working on finding the alternative ideas and addressing them in her essay, when all of a sudden she realized that the alternative was actually better than her original! Right, Rachel?"

Rachel nodded. "It was awful."

I laughed. "Yeah, it's not ideal, especially when you are pretty far along in your drafts. But this is really common; all essay writers face it eventually, realizing in the middle of their essays that their whole claim is off. Rachel, can you report on how you decided to face this crisis?"

Rachel sighed dramatically. "Well, you gave me the choice to try and cover my tracks—not really mentioning the alternative that much, which felt wimpy but easy, or rewriting a bunch of my essay, which felt right but horrible."

"Okay, so before you tell us what you decided, class, will you vote with me? What do you think Rachel should do? The easy way or the right way? How many think the easy way?" A bunch of hands shot up. Laughter filled the room. I said, "Hey, it's a viable option. Okay, how about the right way?" More hands waved in the air. I asked Rachel what she decided to do. She shook her head and groaned.

"Argh! The right way!" Her declaration was met with cheers. I quieted the class and said, "You all may find yourself in this situation as you imagine alternative arguments and interpretations. When you do, you will have to make this same choice."

let your students take the lead in making discoveries. After some discussion, encourage students to look back at their own essay draft and try out some of the new moves they learned.

◆ You might help students strengthen their response to alternative interpretations by teaching them to seek out and closely analyze direct quotes from the text that seem to strongly support their interpretation over the alternative. You could show how phrases like "While many might think . . . they are forgetting the line . . ." can set up this evidence, and coach students to try out this work in the small group.

◆ In the previous session, and in seventh grade, students got a taste of logical thinking as a way to strengthen their arguments. You may also have decided to address logical fallacies with a small group in the last session. Today, many of your more advanced writers could benefit from learning how to deploy logical thinking to counter alternative interpretations. Rather than only analyzing the logic of their own arguments, coach students to flesh out the alternative argument, then look for weaknesses in the logic in order to rebut it. You could use the example from your minilesson, about the kids' meanness, and say something like, "An alternative interpretation is that the kids are less jealous than they are mean, maybe because William does so many mean things, that it seems to show that he's just that type of person, a cruel character, not just acting out of jealousy. But the logic seems to fail a little bit—*if* William is a cruel individual, if this is a trait of his, then he should still be mean at the end. Instead he appears to be reflective, looking down at the ground and letting Margot out of the closet. Therefore, William is not a mean individual, but instead his meanness seems to be motivated by an outside factor, such as the jealousy he feels toward Margot."

Similarly to the last session, this work may be challenging for many of your students. Because of this, a big part of your job during independent writing time today will be to encourage your students to take risks, and to congratulate them for doing so, even if what they produce misses the mark of perfection. As students work, give them the impression that you are proud of them for trying, that the point of their work as writers is sometimes to take a leap of faith and see what happens. After all, this unit is a safe space for your class to try on new moves—in fact, this last year of middle school may be one of the last times they have a teacher who will work with them on the *process* of writing, not just the product. While it is challenging for the best of us to encourage students to try things we are unsure they will be successful with, it is so important that we do so now—so that our writers can find out and push their limits and abilities before they head off to high school. To reach great heights, our students will need us to be their cheerleaders.

As an eighth-grade teacher this identity of cheerleader may come easily—if so, good for you. But this may not be your natural state of being when surrounded by thirty-five thirteen-year-olds. You may believe that being strict and demanding is the best way to be as a teacher of adolescents, or you may use your sarcasm and humor as a way to bond and engage your students. Whatever your natural state, however, you will want to find the cheerleader's voice that feels authentic to you. Our students need praise; they need to know we are proud of their efforts, especially when they are struggling. Without this support, many students will just stop working, or worse, they will believe that this work is not for them. They need us to cheer them on. They need to know we believe in them.

This does not mean that you need to be bright-eyed and bushy-tailed. Many are the classrooms where a demanding teacher is still able to communicate how deeply he loves his students. For him, a simple nod fills his students with pride. What it does mean is that from time to time it will be important for you to take stock of your relationship with your students, particularly when they are working independently, asking yourself if they see you as their cheerleader, their champion, or if they feel more like you are the disapproving judge, tsk-tsking their abilities and shaking your head at their progress.

While every day it is essential that your students see you as their ally, it is all the more important on days like today, when you will be pushing them out of their comfort zones, and asking them to take risks as writers, thinkers, and students. Let them see your metaphorical pom-poms today. Let them know how proud you are of them.

Using Partners to Check Your Work

Channel partnerships to help each other be sure they have addressed the alternative argument fully.

"Writers, most of you have had a chance to try out some alternative arguments in your drafts today, and you've all had a chance during the lesson to try out this kind of thinking. So let's kick it up a notch. One of the hardest parts of doing this kind of work is to really understand the alternative argument, to really get what that argument is saying, and to then argue back directly. For example, say you have been dying for a pet, and you approach your mom to have the discussion. She says no, sorry, you are just not responsible enough. You argue back to her: 'I know you think I'm not responsible enough for a pet but I have saved up a lot of money to get this gerbil.' That counterargument, that you have saved up enough money to get the gerbil, doesn't rebut her point, that you are not responsible enough to take care of a pet. A better argument might be to give examples that demonstrate your responsibility, such as caring for your neighbor's cat when she went on vacation over the holidays.

"So right now, will you point out to your partner a place where you addressed an alternative argument—and partners, could you make sure that the writer has addressed the heart of the alternative argument? One way to do that is to make sure that the writer focuses on the ways the alternative idea isn't as good as their own. In other words—you can check to make sure that they don't go off on any tangents."

As the class worked I listened into a few partnerships. Glen was saying to Lucas, "You said the other idea would be that the story is about how everyone deserves justice but then you didn't say why that's not as good an idea." I piped in, "Oh so you are saying that Lucas needs to think about what might be missing in that alternative idea and name it?" Glen nodded.

> Other people would say you sucseed in life not because you try hard because you have luck. But, with those people I dont agree. I believe that If you try hard enough you will sucseed. I found an example to prove my statment. Inthe novel Harry is afraid to go and fight Malfoy in the middle of the night. He tries hard to face his fears. He beleives in himself. That wasnt about luck, it was about Harry being brave and facing his fears.

FIG. 7–1   Stav's alternative argument about the nature of success

REVISING YOUR DRAFT

"For homework tonight, you'll want to finish revising your draft. This means that right now, you need to plan out really purposefully what needs to happen tonight—what do you need to take home with you? How much time do you need? I could see some of you needing some time to thread today's and the previous lessons through the rest of your essay. Others of you might need to be sure you have quotes embedded in your essays, while still some of you might really need to read your essay from the beginning, looking for gaps or places you need to revise. Take a moment now to think about your plan and write it down. You'll have some time, first thing tomorrow, to show your partner what you accomplished. But above all else, please make sure you come to school with a revised essay."

Session 8

Editing Using All You Know

ear Teachers,

From time to time we'll write a letter to you with some suggestions for the day rather than writing out in detail what we've done. We hope this will give you a welcome opportunity to get your own curriculum-writing feet beneath you. When you do design your own minilesson, with just some scaffolding from us, you'll be able to especially tailor it to your students.

In this session, you'll set up students to effectively edit their work before putting on their final stamp of approval. To prepare for today's session, you'll want to have read their writing with an eye on who needs what when it comes to conventions—and to make sure that in your whole-class lesson, you are teaching toward a *majority* need. (You can of course pull small groups of students during independent writing time to address any minority needs.) You may have done this as the unit was progressing, or before the unit even began. Some teachers choose to collect students' drafts, looking them over and sorting for small groups. Others choose to assess as the students write, looking over their shoulders and recording the needs they see.

MINILESSON

You might begin today's lesson by asking students to talk quickly with their partner about everything they know how to do when it comes time to edit. From there, you can point out that they are experienced at using both editing time and their writing partners to help them find and fix basic errors, like misspelled words and missing punctuation. You'll certainly want to tell them to keep doing that kind of work, while also encouraging them to up the ante by looking for ways to lift the level of their use of conventions. When you deliver your teaching point you might say, "Today I want to remind you that writers use all they know and all they have (relying on the resources at their disposal) to put the final touches on their drafts. But I also want to teach you that when writers edit, they don't

COMMON CORE STATE STANDARDS: W.8.1, W.8.5, W.8.9a, RL.8.1, RL.8.2, RL.8.3, RL.8.4, RL.8.10, SL.8.1, L.8.1, L.8.2, L.8.3, L.8.6

simply fix a misspelled word or add a missing period. Instead, they continue to look for ways to outgrow themselves, this time by lifting the level of their conventions."

To demonstrate your teaching point, you might first show students how you were careful to fix errors in your writing. You could display an enlarged page from your writing that contains various corrections, quickly walking through the section with your class, pointing out the errors that you noticed, emphasizing for them that you found these edits by reading carefully. You'll want to note how you read carefully, maybe aloud, looking for errors and fixing them as you read. If you feel your class needs more demonstration, you could also display a section of your essay that has not been edited, and go through a bit of that text together, urging students to give you a thumbs up when they see a misspelled word, or a misuse of punctuation, or even a clumsily written sentence. Then you might sit back, arms folded across your chest and claim, "Great, I'm finished!" before shaking your head and saying something like, "You know, I think I'm letting myself off the hook too easily here. I think I can use tools I have—like the seventh-grade Argument Writing Checklist I have already used for my essay, and I could even look at the eighth-grade checklist now to push myself—to help me grow as a writer, by using conventions in more sophisticated ways."

From there, you might display the conventions section of the checklist alongside your enlarged, edited writing and notice that the checklist expects you to use internal punctuation appropriately within sentences and when citing sources. You might first think aloud about what that *really* means, perhaps mentioning that sometimes writers clarify what they mean by adding more to a sentence with an appositive, or by tucking in an aside within parentheses. Brainstorm a list of all the different types of internal punctuation you know, asking students to help by calling out what they know, too, as you record each mark on a one-day chart, along with a reason why writers might use it. You won't have time to truly teach students how to use every type of punctuation, but many will be familiar with the marks, and seeing them on the chart will be enough of a reminder to get some students to incorporate more of them into their pieces. And you will certainly want to show how you incorporate at least a couple into your writing.

Argument Writing Checklist

	Grade 7	NOT YET	STARTING TO	YES!	Grade 8	NOT YET	STARTING TO	YES!
	Structure				**Structure**			
Overall	I laid out a well-supported argument and made it clear that this argument is part of a bigger conversation about a topic/text. I acknowledged positions on the topic or text that might disagree with my own position, but I still showed why my position makes sense.	☐	☐	☐	I laid out an argument about a topic/text and made it clear why my particular argument is important and valid. I stayed fair to those who might disagree with me by describing how my position is one of several and making it clear where my position stands in relation to others.	☐	☐	☐
Lead	I interested the reader in my argument and helped them to understand the backstory behind it. I gave the backstory in a way that got the reader ready to see my point.	☐	☐	☐	After hooking the reader, I provided specific context for my own as well as another position(s), introduced my position, and oriented readers to the overall line of argument I planned to develop.	☐	☐	☐
	I made it clear to readers what my piece will argue and forecasted the parts of my argument.	☐	☐	☐				
Transitions	I used transitions to link the parts of my argument. The transitions help the reader follow from part to part and make it clear when I am stating a claim or counterclaim, giving a reason, or offering or analyzing evidence. These transitions include terms such as *as the text states, this means, another reason, some people may say, but, nevertheless,* and *on the other hand.*	☐	☐	☐	I used transitions to lead the reader across parts of the text and to help the reader note how parts of the text relate back to earlier parts. I used phrases such as *now some argue, while this may be true, it is also the case that, despite this, as stated earlier, taken as a whole, this is significant because, the evidence points to,* and *by doing so . . .*	☐	☐	☐
Ending	In my conclusion, I reinforced and built on the main point(s) in a way that makes the entire text a cohesive whole. The conclusion may reiterate how the support for my claim outweighed the counterclaim(s), restate the main points, respond to them, or highlight their significance.	☐	☐	☐	In the conclusion, I described the significance of my argument for stakeholders, or offered additional insights, implications, questions, or challenges.	☐	☐	☐

You might take a sample of your mentor essay, like this excerpt from the one used in this unit:

By the middle of the story the reader begins to see that the children, in their painful jealousy, hurt Margot with words and with force. First they mock her poetry and her memories, claiming she never did see the sun. Then they shove her. Finally, they lock her in a closet so she won't see the sun.

First you will want to name that you are already doing some nice things with your punctuation. For instance, your use of more complex sentences and interspersing short sentences gives your writing a variety of sentence structures that you will want to point out to your students who might use this text as a mentor for their own sentence variety. Then you might look for places in your writing where you could say a little more that might help clarify what you are saying, either by explaining things a bit further or giving a little more pertinent backstory. Once you have found a place, model how you choose what kinds of punctuation you will use and then revise your writing, perhaps to look a little more like this:

By the middle of the story the reader begins to see that the children, in their painful jealousy, hurt Margot with words and with force. First they mock her poetry and her memories, claiming she never did see the sun **(even though in their hearts, they know she did, and it is killing them with jealousy)**. Then they shove her. Finally, they lock her in a closet so she won't see the sun.

You'll likely invite students to help, though you'll probably want them to think silently at first as they watch you, so you can do the initial heavy lifting. You could show how you reread your writing, looking for where you might use parentheses to quietly tuck a little more information into one of your sentences to further convey meaning; or dashes to add information you want to spotlight; or a colon to add a *list* of information you want to spotlight. In addition to adding more information, you might need to rewrite sentences to effectively incorporate new punctuation, and you'll want to highlight this fact for students, so they aren't simply looking for places in their writing to plop in a semicolon. You'll want to emphasize for students that the end goal is not to use new punctuation for the sake of using new punctuation; rather, it is to use new punctuation for the sake of enhancing meaning.

The active engagement in this session is a good time for partners to begin the work of helping each other see errors in their writing. Have students switch essays with their partners, and while still with you in a meeting area, have them read aloud each other's first paragraph, discussing the misspellings and punctuation errors they see. This will be a chance for you to notice those students who shrug and say everything is fine when you know from your initial assessment that they need more support. You will confer with these students soon—for now, just notice who is able to see errors and who is not.

You might also use the active engagement to give students time to study their own pieces alongside the conventions section of the Argument Writing Checklist, looking for places where they, too, might incorporate new internal punctuation to clarify and emphasize meaning—and to strengthen their positions by sounding more knowledgeable. You'll want to circulate and coach students as they work. As you see individuals engaged and successful, you might one by one send them off to finish putting the final touches on their pieces at their seats.

As students settle into their independent writing, you might first work with those still in the meeting area and struggling with the day's lesson. Perhaps editing for basic conventions is the most pressing need for them, and rather than coaching them to vary their punctuation, you might remind them how to use an editing checklist to fix errors. You can coach them to reread their pieces several times, each time with a different lens. You might also ask them to identify what is particularly hard for them when it comes to using correct conventions (Do they struggle to identify misspelled words? Are they unsure when to use a comma?), so you can partner them up with a peer editor who can help them find and fix those kinds of mistakes.

You might go on to gather other students, showing them how, as they work to incorporate a variety of punctuation, they might also use mentor sentences to help them vary the length and complexity of their own sentences. To prepare for this work, you might gather three to four very different sentences (consider length, complexity, punctuation), write them on a piece of paper, and make photocopies to distribute to students in a small group. You might begin by picking one of the sentences to use as a mentor and together, first study the sentence and name its parts, then rewrite one of your sentences to mirror its structure. From there, you can coach each student as she or he tries similar work—first studying a sentence, then rewriting one of their own. Students may or may not choose to study every sentence on the handout when they return to their seats, but encourage them to rewrite at least a couple of their own sentences to make their writing more varied and sophisticated. You can also encourage them to look for and emulate mentor sentences on their own in the future (perhaps the next time they sit down to read), jotting in their notebook ones that strike them as particularly beautiful or interesting. Jeff Anderson's books *Everyday Editing* (2007) and *Mechanically Inclined* (2005) are great resources to support you in this work.

You might also use this time to rally and organize students who can effectively act as peer editors. Invite them to set up their own coaching table or corner of the room where their peers can come for particular help. Perhaps you prep one or two students to sit in an area and offer help with spelling; others to offer help with end punctuation; still others to offer help around punctuating quotations. You might then encourage certain students to visit a table or two based on their particular needs.

Today's mid-workshop teaching could be used to remind students that all authors have an editor that fixes lingering mistakes before the piece goes to publication. You can tell students you want to give them the opportunity to receive similar support. You might explain that peer editors have set up shop, each one offering assistance in a particular area, and then invite students to visit one or more tables as they deem necessary for themselves. Or you might instead invite students to work with their partners, giving one another's writing a thorough read whenever they feel ready for a second pair of eyes. Students could also use this time with their partner to focus on how they are lifting the level of their punctuation. Have them take a few moments to share their revisions, first reading aloud their initial sentence and then their revised version, making sure to read in a way that allows their partner to hear the punctuation changes.

As they work, voice over, emphasizing for the class how the changes in punctuation both deepen the meaning as well as make the writers sound more knowledgeable and sophisticated, and hence, like more of an authority on the subject.

As you wrap up the bend, you'll probably want to give students the opportunity to reflect on the work they've done so far in the unit and to look ahead to their upcoming work. You can ask students to pull out their copies of the seventh- and eighth-grade Argument Writing Checklist and say, "As you look back on the things that you've accomplished with this one essay, this is a great chance to celebrate and notice the ways you've grown as an essayist. You'll want to keep those strengths in mind as you move to other essays."

Then push your class to look ahead by pointing out the eighth-grade checklist and its opportunities for goal-setting. You might say, "We've worked with the seventh-grade Argument Writing Checklist already in this unit, and I saw that a number of you were using the eighth-grade checklist as well, to guide your editing today. Now that you have the seventh- and eighth-grade checklists side by side, you can use them to think ahead to the next part of this unit, when you'll be writing a new essay; you can set some goals for what you want to do, right from the starting gate. Maybe it will be something you're starting to do well and want to do better now, or perhaps it will be something on the checklists that you haven't yet tried."

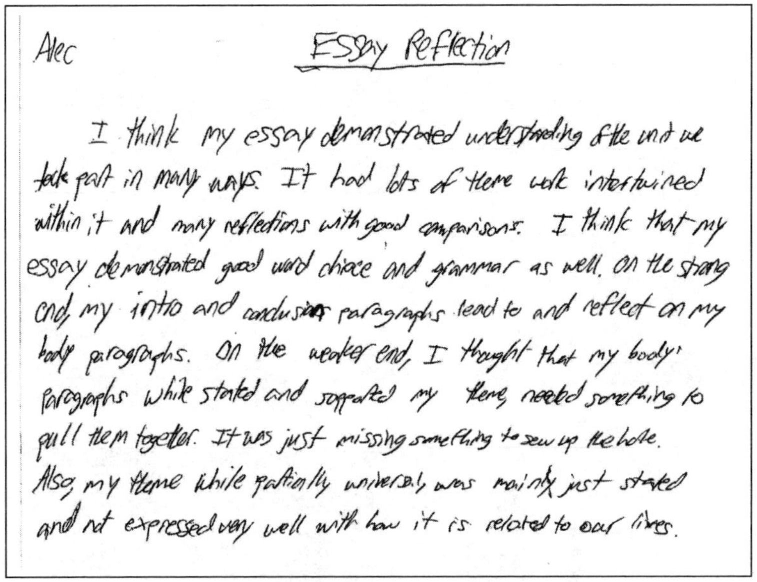

Alec

Essay Reflection

I think my essay demonstrated understanding of the unit we took part in many ways. It had lots of theme work intertwined within it and many reflections with good comparisons. I think that my essay demonstrated good word choice and grammar as well. On the strong end, my intro and conclusion paragraphs lead to and reflect on my body paragraphs. On the weaker end, I thought that my body paragraphs while stated and supported my theme, needed something to pull them together. It was just missing something to sew up the hole. Also, my theme while partially universal, was mainly just stated and not expressed very well with how it is related to our lives.

FIG. 8–1 Alec reflects on his essay.

You'll want to give students the chance to reflect. If there's time, you could continue, adding, "Will you spend a few minutes with your partner pointing out what you've noticed and what goals you're setting? If you have set a goal to try something you haven't tried before, see if your partner has tried it—maybe he or she can be your coach as you embark on this new work."

Good luck!
Kate and Katy

Noticing How an Author Tends to Write

IN THIS SESSION, you'll teach students that literary essayists look for craft moves that the author uses repeatedly. Then, essayists write a bit about why they think the author chooses to write in that way, and what effect those craft moves have on the text.

GETTING READY

✔ Link to the photograph of a woman with her children during the Great Depression, http://www.loc.gov/pictures/resource/fsa.8b29516/ (Google search term "Dorothea Lange Migrant Mother"), or another photograph that students can use to discuss message (see Connection).

✔ "Narrative Writers Use Techniques Such As . . ." and "Narrative Writers Aim Toward Goals Such As . . ." charts (see Teaching)

✔ Students' copies and teacher copy of the class-shared text, "All Summer in a Day" (see Teaching)

✔ An entry from your writer's notebook (see Teaching)

✔ Texts that students have been using to write their essays (see Active Engagement and Share)

✔ "How to Write an Author's Craft Essay" anchor chart (see Link)

COMMON CORE STATE STANDARDS: W.8.1, W.8.3.b,d; W.8.9.a, W.8.10, RL.8.1, RL.8.2, RL.8.3, RL.8.4, SL.8.1, SL.8.2, L.8.1, L.8.2, L.8.3, L.8.4

THE SECOND BEND OF THIS UNIT teaches students that essayists sometimes write entire essays in which they focus on the way an author uses a particular craft move to create an effect or accentuate a theme. While in the last bend, you coached your students to notice craft as evidence of an author's intended theme, now you will be teaching your students to write essays in which their entire focus is on a discussion of the craft in a text, and exploring the intentions behind those choices. Assuming you and your colleagues have followed the curricular pathways outlined in this series, your students will be more than ready to tackle this challenge. They have written about an author's craft before—both in sixth grade as a way to find more evidence for their essays and in seventh grade as a way to powerfully reflect on books they are reading.

What they have not done before, however, is to center an essay upon the craft that they notice—writing a claim that focuses on a few moves the author makes, and then using what they know about essays to build their argument that these craft moves are significant. This is important work to embrace as an eighth-grade teacher, as high-stakes assessments and high school classes often ask students to do this work. A deep study of craft can't be relegated to reading or test prep alone, as ultimately students need to use writing as the vehicle for conveying their insights. This bend aims to give students the time to practice and grow these important academic skills.

For this bend, you will probably want your students to return to the same novel and to work in the same partnerships as they did during the previous portion of the unit. However, if you want to nudge a cluster of your students to tackle especially challenging work, you could see if they'd be willing to try this second bend with a new text, which would then mean that they needed to redo the work of Bend I on their own as they focus on the work of Bend II. Of course, there may be a few students whose partnerships need to be altered or whose books aren't well written enough to bear this scrutiny, in which case you can make revisions now. Be sure, however, that students are again writing about a text they know well and one they can read with ease.

Noticing How an Author Tends to Write

CONNECTION

Use a photograph to jog students' thinking about how creators of all kinds of texts make deliberate choices to get their message across.

"Writers, take a look at this photograph . . . and think for a moment. What message do you think this photographer is sending?" I asked, as I projected the famous photo of a woman with her children during the Great Depression. "Turn and talk." The image can be found at http://www.loc.gov/pictures/resource/fsa.8b29516/ (Google search term "Dorothea Lange Migrant Mother").

The class erupted in conversation. I listened as Myah told her partner, Kiara, "She's sad," and Kiara added, "She's protecting her children."

Voicing over the hubbub, I said, "Tell each other what exactly it is you see in the photograph that supports your belief that this is the message the photographer is sending."

I pulled in to listen as Kiara and Myah continued to talk. Kiara thought for another moment and said, "The expression on her face. And the way her hand is on her face. And like, the color of it."

Myah jumped in again, "Yeah and how it's like you can see all the details like an HD TV."

"Writers, the evidence you are mentioning doesn't pertain to the *content* of the photo, but to the *craft* of it—to the way the mother's face is turned to the camera, to the way the kids are turned away on either side of her. You are right that the photographer *could* have arranged the picture differently and it would have sent a different message." Then I added, "As literary essayists, it will pay off for you to remember that authors, like photographers, often convey more through their craft than through their content. And remember—authors, like photographers, do things on purpose. An author doesn't throw in a simile or repeat a phrase for no reason. The author uses technique, just as the photographer does when she turns the mother's face this way or that, to convey a message."

By referencing the ways in which a photographer uses technique to highlight a theme, you spotlight the way that authors do the same thing. One of the things we know about teaching for transference is that teaching across modalities helps to cement a concept. Just as important, using images helps to engage your students.

Notice that we are not suggesting you harvest all the insights your students can offer. Time is of the essence, and the really important thing is that students had a moment to engage in this work.

Set up the work for this bend, namely that you are beginning a new and important kind of literary essay today.

"Today you are going to begin writing a brand-new essay, one that will prepare you even more for your work in high school, and beyond. Today, we are going to start studying the Author's Craft essay, and I am really excited. Not only is it great to flex and grow your essay-writing muscles by trying out lots of different types of essay writing, but examining and analyzing author's craft is just a really interesting thing to do.

"As essayists, it is wise to approach texts knowing from the start that you are going to look at the author's craft and then figure out how these deliberate craft moves advance the author's purpose. You'll be looking for how the crafting techniques show what the author intended for readers to take away from the text. Literary essayists teach readers about the craft moves they notice in a text."

Introducing the chart on this page will broaden your students' view of the craft that they notice in a text.

❖ **Name the teaching point.**

"So, writers, today I want to teach you that when writing literary essays, you have choices. One way to write an essay is to put forward an idea that the story suggests—a theme. Another way to write a literary essay is to focus on the craft moves an author tends to use, and to write an essay where you argue that the author's craft choices have a specific purpose or pattern."

TEACHING

Show students how you begin by choosing a scene at the start of your text, searching for craft moves, similarly to how you did in Bend I.

"So the good news is you all know how to do the first step of this work—you just need to reread a bit of your texts and see what kinds of craft moves you notice. You did this last week when we looked for craft as evidence for the themes we were writing about.

"I could just use the stuff I found last week, but I'm going to take another look and see what I can see today. To mix it up, I am going to try and focus on a different part of the text—a scene or character that I didn't spend much time on before. I'm thinking that maybe I could focus on the scenes with the sun this time, since for my last essay I focused a whole lot on the rain. Let's look together at this scene at the beginning of 'All Summer in a Day.' It's the part where Bradbury is describing the children's seemingly subconscious recollections of the sun. Just like I did before, I am going to reread this scene closely, and examine the crafting decisions he made. To look for craft, I am going to use a chart you all used in seventh grade, 'Narrative Writers Use Techniques Such As. . . .'

"So, like you did last year, I am going to read, using this chart—which is really a list of narrative techniques similar to the one you used when we looked for craft last week. I think this chart will help us to focus on some craft moves we may otherwise miss . . . let's try it." I read it aloud.

Narrative Writers Use Techniques Such As...

Flashback & flashforward	Multiple plot lines	Inner thinking
Dialogue	Revealing actions	Multiple points of view
1st person narrator	Reader knows MORE than the character	Description
Metaphor	Tone	Symbolism

They were all nine years old, and if there had been a day, seven years ago, when the sun came out for an hour and showed its face to the stunned world, they could not recall. Sometimes, at night, she heard them stir, in remembrance, and she knew they were dreaming and remembering gold or a yellow crayon or a coin large enough to buy the world with. She knew they thought they remembered a warmness, like a blushing in the face, in the body, in the arms and legs and trembling hands.

I thought out loud, listing a few craft moves across my fingers. "Hmm . . . The first thing I notice is that Bradbury is saying the sun is like a yellow crayon, and like a coin. He uses similes and metaphors. And he also talks about how warm the sun is, like a blushing in the face, and that it makes your whole body tremble. That's him using descriptive language. I know from earlier in this unit that I can then think about *why* he is making those choices—what the author's purpose is. You used a chart for that as well last year, remember? It was the 'Narrative Writers Aim Toward Goals Such As . . .' chart.

"So with this chart we can think—*why* did Ray Bradbury use those metaphors, that descriptive language? We can look at this chart and see what fits. What do you think?"

Rachel spoke up, "I guess he wrote it like that to . . . um . . ." She looked at the chart. "Oh. To show the character's motivation!"

Rochelle added on, "And also totally to raise the stakes! Because you see how much the children want the sun."

Show students how you skim through the text to look for patterns in the craft an author is using.

"So now I am going to skim through the rest of the text, lingering on places where I think I might find more examples of these craft moves—similes and metaphors and descriptive language. This means I have to be a little strategic—what kinds of scenes should I linger on? I could choose similar *kinds* of scenes—like setting description in my case—or scenes that have something in common like scenes between two characters. For now, I am going to look for parts where the narrator is describing the sun, since I haven't really thought too much about that yet, and I'm interested to see what I find."

I demonstrated skimming the text with my finger, scanning the page for a second. "Okay, so this scene where he describes the sun coming out is interesting. There is a bunch of description here; it says the sun 'was the color of flaming bronze,' and that the jungle 'burned with sunlight.' Oh! and there it says the sun burnt the children 'like a warm iron.' Another simile!"

If you have a document camera or Smart Board, it will benefit your class to see you do the actual skimming work involved in this lesson. While your class has had experience identifying and reflecting on craft moves before, this work of locating other examples of the same craft move in a text may be new for them, and they could use a visual of you skimming, then pausing, reading a bit, and discovering a pattern. If you do not have a way to project your text, then be sure to highlight for your class when you are stopping, and what you are noticing.

I moved my finger down the page again until I came to another scene. "Here when the children are playing in the sun, there's a simile when it says the children played 'like animals escaped from their caves,' and there is a whole list of descriptive actions, like running and falling and squinting and breathing and listening and looking. This part isn't describing the sun, but it is describing the effect the sun has on the kids. And through it all are similes and descriptive language. All of this, I think, raises the stakes in the story because it shows how desirable the sun is to the kids."

Debrief the steps you took, and channel students to see how writing could help you grow your thinking.

"So to look for what an author tends to do with their craft, first I chose a spot to study, naming the craft moves I saw. Then I skimmed the text, pausing in places that made sense, looking for other examples of these craft moves. Of course, it would help me if I wrote some of my thinking down. It is especially important to think a little about why the author was doing these things, and what effect these moves have on the text—work you have also done before. Remember that you can use the chart you used last year to remind you of ways to think about this.

"Last night I used this thinking—and this chart—to help me, and I wrote an entry in my writer's notebook to show you. Use it as inspiration for your work today."

> Bradbury uses metaphor throughout "All Summer in a Day." He describes the sun "like a lemon," and "like a flower," and when the children are playing in the sun he describes them "like animals escaped from their caves." One effect of this device is to create a vivid setting in the reader's mind. When he says the sun is like a lemon, I know exactly what that looks like, just how bright and yellow it shines. Another effect is to raise the stakes by showing the sun as something so good, and maybe even a little wild. For example, when the children get into the sun they act like freed animals–this simile really shows how the sun frees the children from their own caves. This raises the stakes because it shows the sun as something so desirable that the children might do anything to get it.

ACTIVE ENGAGEMENT

Channel students to try these steps in their own stories, getting started by working with their partners.

"I always find this work way more helpful with a partner. Working with other people helps me see so much more than I can alone! Right now, work with your partner to discover what craft moves you see your author using. Start by choosing a scene or character to focus on, and examine the craft moves you notice. Then work together to skim some other parts of the text to see if any of those moves fit a pattern. Get to work."

As students worked, I coached partnerships and groups to zero in on a scene, saying, "You could focus on a scene at the beginning of the text that seems like it has a lot of description," or "Sometimes I just go right to a scene I really love. Often the reason why I love scenes is because they are written so well."

While certainly your students will not have memorized these texts, it is important that you push your class to hold more of it in their heads—to know where scenes are, and to recall certain moments in the text, even if it takes a second to find them.

While often you will write in front of your students, in this case I show a prewritten entry. This is because this entry work is work the class has done before, and is meant to be a reminder and a vision of what their work could become today. Showing a full prewritten essay is a time-saver, but will not support the students' learning as much as demonstration.

I also helped those students who still struggled to name craft moves, coaching, "First just point to a place that you think might be a craft move. Then you can work with your partner to name it. Use the narrative techniques and goals charts as a reference if you need to."

Listening in, I offered encouragement and support until two minutes or so had passed. Then I brought the class together. "Nice, nice job helping each other today. Winnie, can you tell us a bit about what you and Jonathan noticed?"

Winnie spoke so softly that we all leaned in a bit closer. "Well. We saw this short sentence. So we looked for other short sentences. And we saw them all over the place."

I nodded, "Nice. Did you two have a chance to talk about why the author would do that?" Jonathan raised his hand and spoke when I nodded. "I think he did that to make us pay attention to that part. Like we can't help but read that sentence so much because it stands out."

LINK

Guide students toward the craft analysis they will be undertaking, allowing them choice as to how they will take on the work.

"So today I'd like you to study the patterns of craft your author uses in the text you have read. To do this, you will need to think a bit about how you work most efficiently. You could work alone, with one partner, or with a group. But be aware, I am going to be paying attention to how much you get done today, so be sure to make the smartest choice for yourself. You can use this chart to help you in your work today." I revealed a chart I had made earlier.

How to Write an Author's Craft Essay

- Collect entries on the author's craft.

  - Choose a spot in the text to study and name a few craft moves you see the author using.

  - Look for patterns of craft across the text in similar scenes.

"After you have chosen how you will work today, go ahead and find a good place in the room to get started. I think a good goal for your work today would be to get two pages written in your notebooks, where you write long about a few different craft moves you see the author using over and over."

I often invite specific students to share what they are thinking—but my invitations aren't random. While listening in on student talk, I can find students to highlight whose work will push the rest of the class, supporting their work and my lesson. If I hear discussion that suggests big misconceptions, I can be sure to meet with those students during the workshop.

Of course you could also direct students to work alone or with others, depending on what you think will support kids best. The reason we offered this choice to students here is to consciously provide opportunities for kids to make their own decisions, and see the results from that. Next year, in high school, it will help if students know how they work best so they can more readily seek out private space, or a study partner, as they see fit.

Helping Students Hold On to Your Teaching

TODAY YOUR STUDENTS will again be writing entries about the texts that they've been studying all along. One of the important things will be for you to clarify in your own mind (and then convey to students) the differences between an entry and an essay. You'll want students to know this is writing-to-learn. It is not meant to be written in a declarative, authoritative voice. This is a time for musing, for sentences that start, "I'm not sure, but maybe . . ." and are followed by sentences that might start, "Then again, perhaps it's . . ." or "I wonder. . . . Could it be that . . . ?" You might think about differences like those below.

Qualities of Good Writing-to-Think about Texts	Qualities of Good Essay Writing
Let the text teach you how to respond.	Use a structure that will allow your reader to see your big idea and supporting ideas and details.
Use different structures, including graphics, to capture your ideas.	
Write long, in a speculative tone, to try to put into words ideas that start out partly formed.	Write with a formal, authoritative tone.
	Pick and choose, selecting evidence and details that best support your ideas.
Move between multiple specific details and big ideas.	

As you think through—and ensure that students see—these differences, it may be helpful for you to glance over the seventh-grade *Writing About Reading* unit. Assuming that your students' seventh-grade teacher taught this unit, the strategies that they learned for writing about reading will be helpful for them to reprise in eighth grade, and knowing a bit about those techniques will help you support students in carrying their knowledge from one year to the next. In that unit, your students studied some specific strategies for good writing-to-think about reading, including:

◆ Using graphics to respond to texts

◆ Writing long to capture ideas that may start out half-formed

◆ Writing to connect story elements

◆ Letting the text teach you how to respond to it

As you confer, you might refine these strategies by researching students who are writing about craft in particular ways. It's important to learn why a student has chosen to, say, write long from a Post-it®, or create a Venn diagram. If the student has a purpose, you might reflect upon how the form of their writing helps meet that purpose,

MID-WORKSHOP TEACHING
Motivating Students to Write More

"Writers, one thing that is important to remember is that more writing is often better than laboring over little bits of it—especially when you are collecting, like you are right now. Today, I don't want you worrying about whether your ideas are perfect or not—right now your job is to find as much and write as much as possible.

"Take Jonathan—he is really cooking with gas here—he has three entries written about different craft moves he sees as patterns in his text! Let's get a sense of how this is going for people—how many of you have three entries like Jonathan?" A few hands shot up proudly.

"And how many have two?" More hands went up. "One?" Most of the remaining hands filled the air.

"Okay, so while more isn't always better, when we are collecting for something it often is. See how many entries you can collect by the end of the period. I know Jonathan is competitive, so why don't you see if you can beat him." I winked at Jonathan and sent the class back to work.

BNE

In the novel The Maze Runner, Thomas is constantly seeking recognition. He is frequently asking questions. He doubts himself and doesn't have the confidence to actually believe in his own choices & make things happen. But as the novel evolves, the reader learns that Thomas's questions to others soon become statements. The question marks that constantly appeared soon fade away and become periods to his own answers. I think the author purposely made Thomas seem confused and out of place to really highlight the transition that he makes from not ambiguous to dignified. The reader really gets connected & attached to Thomas's story developing as the book goes on.

(James Dashner)

FIG. 9–1 Celine writes about James Dashner's craft moves in *The Maze Runner*.

and perhaps suggest a tip to strengthen that work. However, if the student seems to be working more randomly, choosing a style of notebook entry without a reason, you might coach students to consider the possibilities for their entries and to take a more playful stance in their notebook.

As in Session 3 in the first bend, there will be students on this day that will need your support in identifying craft moves and thinking more deeply about why the author chose to write that way. When these students seem stuck, help them as you did before to locate a place where they feel like they see the writing pop, and then help them to match what they are seeing to the name of that craft move. You may also direct their attention to the resources they have to help them, from the craft chart referenced in the lesson and brought forward from their seventh-grade work to their own entries from earlier in the unit. However, if these are the same students who struggled earlier, you might want to think a bit about what is not working for them in your classroom, what the factors are that may be causing them to have a tough time holding on to the lessons you are teaching them. While certainly there is not an expectation that your students remember every single word you utter, it is equally true that you want them to hold on to some of what you teach in your conferences and small groups.

If you feel that one or more of your students are habitually letting lessons slip off of them like water off of a duck, try addressing the issue head on. Pull the students you are worried about together and have a discussion about how they see these conferences and small groups, what they add to their writing and reading, and what might be getting in the way of their taking them more seriously or being able to remember what was taught. Often students will tell you that they are paying attention but have trouble keeping track of a conference after it is over. You can help these students to hold on to teaching by having them take notes on their conference in little assignment boxes at the corners of their notebook pages, or in their student agendas, or wherever makes sense for them. We have found that sometimes it is simply the act of you pulling a student aside and saying, "Hey, I really think these conferences are important," that changes their attitudes about them.

This is also a powerful time to check in on your partnerships, and how your students are supporting each other when you are not there. Listen in to some of the duos that have chosen to work together in this session, and see if they are both being supportive of each other's work while at the same time pushing each other to greater heights. If not, you might revisit some of the strategies you taught in the very first unit, like asking detailed questions about specific goals, giving honest, specific feedback from a reader's perspective, or using each other to rehearse parts before writing them.

Exceptional Craft Moments

Point out to students the power of the exception, and give them an example from the text you have been studying.

"Writers, I know that during this session I have pushed you to look for the craft moves that you see repeated in a text, so that you can start to think about what the author tends to do as a writer. I think many of you see how powerful this can be—and how much closer it brings you to the text. But there is something else that is just as powerful—and it is the exact opposite of what I taught you. While patterns of craft are important to notice, so are stand-alone exceptions—times when the author does something that they never or rarely do again in the text.

"Like in 'All Summer in a Day' when the kids finally see the sun, finally get outside to play and bask in it, Bradbury describes what they did with a run-on sentence of sorts, several ideas, linked with an *and*."

> *But they were running and turning their faces up to the sky and feeling the sun on their cheeks like a warm iron . . .*

"This run-on almost shows an urgency, an urgency because the kids only have two hours to enjoy the sun, and then that's it, for seven more years. How much can they squeeze in, how much can they do, in these two hours? This is not a pattern of Bradbury's, but the very fact that it stands out so much makes it super interesting to study."

Channel students to look for exceptions in their own texts with a partner.

"Can you right now see if you and your partner can find some moments in your text that you think might be standout exceptions? Try it."

Lucas and Glen were having a tough time. I went over to them and said, "Look, you don't have to find an exception right now to be successful. You could just go into the story and notice something you missed before, and think a little about why the author did that. Don't get hung up on its being the only time the author wrote like that." Lucas looked relieved and picked up the story he was reading.

ANALYZING CRAFT: PATTERNS AND EXCEPTIONS

"Tonight for homework I am going to ask you to keep on with this work, trying for two more pages of entries in your notebooks. It will be up to you whether it makes sense to mostly look for exceptions or patterns or both. The important thing is that you come in tomorrow with lots to say to your partners about the craft moves you see your author using, and what you think the significance of those choices might be."

The Power of Symbolism

IN THIS SESSION, you'll teach students that literary essayists are often on the lookout for one especially powerful craft move that authors use to great effect—symbols. You will teach students to look for this device in their own texts and to write long to discover the deeper meaning behind the symbols they discover.

GETTING READY

✔ Students' writer's notebooks and pens (see Teaching, Active Engagement, and Link)

✔ Copies of the class-shared text "All Summer in a Day" (see Teaching and Active Engagement) 🔾

✔ Your own writer's notebook (see Teaching)

✔ "How to Write an Author's Craft Essay" anchor chart (see Link and Share) 🔾

✔ Your own possible author's craft essay claims, enlarged for the class to see (see Share)

COMMON CORE STATE STANDARDS: W.8.1, W.8.4, W.8.9.a, W.8.10, RL.8.1, RL.8.2, RL.8.3, RL.8.4, SL.8.1, SL.8.2, L.8.1, L.8.2, L.8.3, L.8.4

T HIS SESSION AIMS TO SUPPORT your students in carrying forward their learning and applying it to new situations, new texts. If your school has adopted this series, then last year your students learned how to write about the symbols in a text in powerful ways. While here you will help your students to practice the skill of writing about symbols in texts in slightly more sophisticated ways, much of the work of this session is devoted to getting your class up to speed on this essential craft move quickly and efficiently.

As you teach today, you will ask your students to take notes on the steps you take, ensuring that they are paying attention to the specifics of your demonstration. In addition, you will teach your students to look for symbols, hoping to condense work that last year or in years past took multiple days. In this you will be reviewing the work of the past for your class, without taking a step backward. Similarly, instead of just repeating the work they did last year, you will look for places to lift the level of the thinking they are doing around symbols—pushing them to articulate what the author's purpose may have been in including that layer in the text.

As students work today, they'll be writing entries in their notebooks. Expect—and push for—at least two entries during this class period, each roughly a page long. As with the last session, you'll want to be clear that you're not looking for students to write in a formal essay structure at this point—you'll want to distinguish between writing-to-think and essay writing, looking for students to be exploring ideas rather than declaring them finished. You'll channel students to put a special emphasis on symbolism, but not to abandon the other craft work they began previously.

Then, at the end of this session, you will set your class up to work on developing a few possible claims for this new iteration of essay, since in the next session they will practice a few ways their drafts could go. Because of this, your focus is on getting your students working quickly and with high volume—for the more entries they have, the more possible claims they will be able to come in with tomorrow when the rubber hits the road.

The Power of Symbolism

CONNECTION

Explain that there is one craft move every essayist should be on the lookout for.

"Have you guys heard the phrase 'pull your own weight'? My dad would always say that to me when he wanted me to do my chores, or not whine about helping out with my brother, or anything like that. It means that you're doing your part—you are helping the team.

"I remembered that expression the other day when I was thinking about what I would teach you next. In the last session you gathered lots of thinking about patterns of craft moves—and even really powerful stand-alone moves—that might be significant in your texts. But one craft move that most of you *didn't* do a lot of thinking about was symbolism. I want to devote some attention to this today, because symbolism in particular 'pulls its own weight'—it does a lot of work all on its own, so if you can find symbols in your texts, you should probably pay attention."

Name the teaching point.

"Today I want to remind you that literary essayists look out for craft moves that pull their own weight—in particular, symbolism. Looking for symbols, and writing long about them, can help you to write more powerful craft essays."

TEACHING

Remind students of what they know about this topic already.

"So, writers, you already know a lot about how to write and think about symbolism—you did that last year. You know that you can look for symbols, for recurring objects or images or colors, and ask yourself whether they might mean more than they seem to. Do you remember thinking about symbolism in 'The Stolen Party'? Remember the monkey that was at Luciana's birthday party, the monkey that Rosaura was so intrigued by that you decided it might be symbolic of Rosaura's class position? I know that last year you learned about the importance of not just noticing a symbol, but then tracking that symbol throughout the text, noticing multiple meanings, and maybe writing about how the meaning shifts or changes as the story unfolds. This is work that 'pulls its own weight,' for an essayist. Let me show you what I mean."

Note that this lesson is responsive to what the students did or didn't do the day before. I assume many of your students will be like this class—they will avoid the work of symbolism and be drawn to the easier-to-identify work of noticing similes and repetition and descriptive language. If your students have already embraced this work on their own the day before, of course, you will not need this session as is, and may choose another craft move to highlight.

If your students' seventh-grade teachers taught the seventh-grade Writing About Reading unit, they will have studied "The Stolen Party" as an anchor text. If they didn't do this unit or study this text, you will have to refer to a text they have read and studied, specifically with the lens of symbolism. If your students have not had a lesson in symbolism ever before, you will have to decide if this session is appropriate as an introduction to this literary device or if you would rather spend a little time during your reading instruction to focus on that skill.

Demonstrate for students a set of steps they can use to collect writing about symbolism.

"I'm going to try some of this work now, and I want you to note the steps I take. Open up your notebook and when I pause, jot down the step I just took that you could imagine taking another day, with another text.

"So, first I am going to skim back over the text, using my knowledge of the text and of my aim—to look for symbolism—to help me be efficient." I started skimming, and then mused, "I am looking especially for an object or color or image repeated throughout the story. In the last session we studied a bit about the sun, so I'm looking back for those places where the sun is mentioned." I skimmed for a moment. "I'm thinking about how the sun might be a symbol in the story . . . ," and I kept skimming.

I ran my finger quickly down the pages of the story, noting aloud observations like "Wow, even just on the first page the sun comes up a *lot* . . . the author is comparing it to so many good things, like coins and crayons . . . he says that it feels like blushing . . . and wow, later, oh, look, the sun is like a warm iron . . . that sounds nice on a cold day! I definitely think the sun is a symbol here! It is repeated throughout, and it seems to mean more than just itself.

"Okay, note-takers, what is the first step I took? Put it in your own words!" I gave the class a few seconds to jot.

Model the type of notebook entry you'll want your students to collect.

"Okay, so now I probably want to write a little about what the sun might actually symbolize in the text. Remember, when you are analyzing a symbol it's important to think about what the symbol might actually mean, trace that symbol across the text, notice if it is changing at all, and think about how it relates to the theme. Let's see . . ." I picked up a pen and scribbled in my notebook as I spoke. "Bradbury is always comparing the sun to positive things, first small things like crayons, then bigger things like a warm iron. A lot of the comparisons are warm things, too. So, the sun might symbolize something both warm and positive, something that takes care of you or lets you get things done—maybe it symbolizes nourishment! That might fit with the ideas in the story because the kids didn't have that nourishment until this one day.

"Okay, note-takers—what did I just do? Write it down!"

Pausing I said, "Now I want to make sure that I push myself to say not just what this symbol means, but also what job it does in the text. What is Bradbury trying to do by including this symbol? What is he trying to show his readers?" I began to write-in-the-air again. "One effect of using symbolism is that it shows how positive the sun is compared to the usual weather on Venus. Maybe he is using this symbolism to show the opposite of how the kids usually feel—like, usually they're kind of depressed and miserable with the terrible weather, and the sun is like the opposite—it's like vitality, like freedom, like hope even.

"Okay, note-takers—this is the last step—what did I do? When you are done, look over your notes with your partner and see if you missed anything, like any tips I gave that might help you. We are not going to go over the steps together today—so make sure you have a plan you think you can follow."

In this lesson, I want writers to pay attention to the steps I take, and note-taking is a good way to get them to do that. Furthermore, as they get older, your students will need to listen closely for directions, and this lesson aims to help them refine that skill.

You will want to write-in-the-air here—instead of taking the time to actually write these sentences down, speak them aloud. If you want the visual you could always have this entry premade to put on a document camera or on a piece of chart paper afterward.

Of course, this work of asking students to take notes on your steps also allows students to create their own steps in their own words—a level of engagement that will be useful here.

Certainly if your students seem lost at the prospect of taking notes on what you do and then following those steps themselves, you could take the time to go over the steps together. But this lesson aims to push students toward independence, and so instead it might be better for students to feel the burn of needing to figure out what to do next themselves.

ACTIVE ENGAGEMENT

Channel students to try this out with another part of the anchor story.

"Writers, let's test out this work. I am going to do the first step for you and choose something else that seems symbolic for Bradbury. How about we look at the rain? There's a lot about the rain even just on the first page. Remember the steps you took notes on—see how following them helps you out."

As the class worked, I moved around the room pushing students to use the notes they took on the lesson. "What is your first step?" I asked Lauren and Claire, who checked their notes and refocused. As Chris and Shirley started working I pushed them to focus in on the last step they wrote, "Say what effect the symbol has on the story."

Voice over tips as students work.

I paused the class. "Writers, I heard a lot of you talking about what the symbol means—you're really good at that, but don't forget to also look at the newer question—what job does this craft move do in the story? What is the author trying to achieve by putting it in?" Students began talking again.

After a few more minutes, I reconvened the class and recapped what I heard. "So Jared and Flynn dove in, immediately beginning to debate the symbolism, about whether the rain symbolizes sadness or people being hurtful. Then they went off and wrote different entries, each trying to 'prove' that their interpretation was right. They kind of made the steps of my lesson their own, which is neat, because it's working for them."

LINK

Remind students to draw on their repertoire of strategies as they work.

"So, writers, today you'll have an opportunity to continue collecting for this new craft essay. You have some terrific thinking from the last session, but remember, it tends to pay off to look for those craft moves that really pull their own weight—symbolism is one of these. So you might decide that you'll spend some time today working on that, alongside the other craft moves you've been studying in your texts. Today you'll want to collect two or three pages of entries—so you might plan to focus on different parts of your text than you did previously, to make sure you have some new thinking to work on. Right now, in your notebook, jot down a plan for your work. I'll add to our chart to help you with your plan. When you've got your plan down, go for it!"

Voicing over like this during an active engagement serves a similar purpose as a mid-workshop teaching point. It allows you to be responsive to the needs you're identifying in your students, and address some of those classwide needs or misconceptions immediately. Then students can practice the strategy more effectively with the remaining active engagement time. This means, of course, that you will want to adapt this part of the lesson if you find that your students demonstrate a different need.

How to Write an Author's Craft Essay

- Collect entries on the author's craft.
  - Choose a spot in the text to study and name a few craft moves you see the author using.
  - Look for patterns of craft across the text in similar scenes.
- **Focus on powerful craft moves, like symbolism.**

Helping Students Unlock the Power of a Symbol

YOUR FIRST SMALL GROUP TODAY might involve zeroing in on those students who are behind the rest of the class in their knowledge of what exactly a symbol really is, and the effect this device has on texts. These might be students who either were not in your school last year, and so did not go through the *Writing About Reading* unit in seventh grade, or they had a teacher who did not embrace the whole of that work. You won't want to spend more than five or so minutes on any one small group, so it will help to plan your approach in advance, knowing that you won't be able to re-create the whole of the teaching that the rest of your class has had, in one small-group session. You will perhaps gather these students together and tell them a bit about symbolism—perhaps with a quick real-life example, such as how the stuffed lamb you grew up with means more to you than just a stuffed animal—it symbolizes comfort and love. Then you might model how you look for those moves in your mentor text. Next, guide your small group to think a bit about their own texts while they are

still with you. Push them to find places where they see an object, color, or image that keeps arising. You will need to think a bit, too, about the difference between objects that simply keep appearing and those that "feel" symbolic. This is a thin line, and one you may not worry too much about.

As students get started using what you've taught, be aware of the signs of growth, and celebrate them. It may not be that the kids in your small group understand the deep totality of what a symbol is and how to find one in a text. You may find on this day that your students pick out symbols that are pretty literal. A student might, for example, say that Harry's wand in Harry Potter is symbolic, because it is mentioned over and over again. This is not a bad start. (And of course, wands and swords are deeply symbolic across texts and cultures, even though that was not what your student was thinking at the time.) Help your students to see where their thinking goes as they zero in on a

---

MID-WORKSHOP TEACHING **Looking for Patterns across Your Entries**

"Let me give you one more thing you might want to think about. One of the things that essayists often do when they're collecting for this type of writing is to pause frequently to look at what they're gathering and notice whether there are any patterns developing. Maybe there are several craft moves that you notice doing the same kind of work in the text. Maybe there are metaphors that seem to go together in some way. You'll be writing claims soon—in fact, by class time tomorrow you will have some claims written! This kind of pattern thinking will really help with doing that.

"For example, I was working with Kiara and she was showing me an entry she wrote about this cool simile that Veronica Roth used to describe a character in *Divergent*— 'a pale ring of sunlight burns into the clouds like the end of a lit cigarette.' Then Kiara

had another entry about another simile she used, about how someone's smile looks like it was cut into his face with a knife. So Kiara started thinking how interesting it was that both similes were kind of violent—burning, cutting. And she decided to go back and look to see if this is a pattern, if Veronica Roth does this a lot, and maybe this is something important to understand about the book, this pattern of violence almost.

"So, before you get back to work, take a look back at what you've done over the last couple of days. Do you see any patterns? If you do, you might want to think about a way to keep track of the patterns you're seeing—maybe in a new entry, or making up some codes for your different entries. Take a minute to look back and reflect, then dive back in—you don't have much longer to collect entries!"

repeated object. Perhaps your student focusing on Harry's wand will get to the place where he will write that Harry's wand is a symbol for his strength—if this is the case, this student deserves a high-five and some encouragement to keep at it.

Once you've gotten your first small group going, you can circulate quickly to tune in to what the rest of the class is doing. You will want to be on the lookout for those students who are taking to the work of symbols like fish to water, but may struggle to find the purpose behind it. Let these students know that often a symbol tries to represent an emotion, a trait of a character, or their struggle, or even a theme. Help them see, for example, how when you were thinking about the sun in "All Summer in a Day," you thought a bit about how the sun felt, and you got to a place where you were thinking about freedom and hope, and how the sun might be there to represent those ideas in the story.

In any case, spend some time today congratulating and motivating your students to write more. The power of this session is not in your class walking away with one meager entry about one rough draft idea about the symbols in their texts—it lies in a collection of writing that explores many different possibilities. Your students will only produce a bunch of writing and thinking about their texts today if they feel that they might be on the right track—so spend time helping your class to feel that they are, indeed.

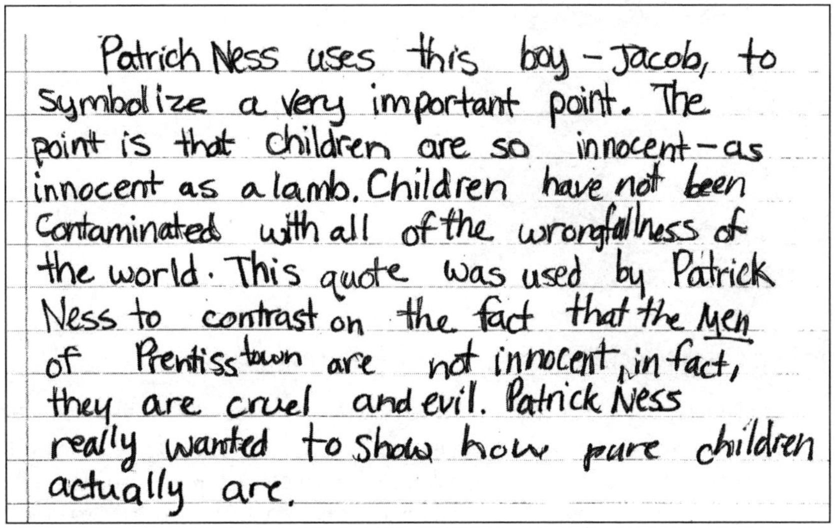

> Patrick Ness uses this boy—Jacob, to symbolize a very important point. The point is that children are so innocent—as innocent as a lamb. Children have not been contaminated with all of the wrongfullness of the world. This quote was used by Patrick Ness to contrast on the fact that the Men of Prentisstown are not innocent, in fact, they are cruel and evil. Patrick Ness really wanted to show how pure children actually are.

FIG. 10–1 Rachel writes about how author Patrick Ness uses the boy, Jacob, as a symbol in The *Knife of Never Letting Go*.

Writing Claims about Craft

Help students to develop strong claims for craft essays.

"Writers! You are at an important crossroads for this next essay! Tomorrow you are going to walk in here with some claims that might make great craft essays. Before you do, let's talk a little about what these claims might sound like. Here are two claims I drafted last night about 'All Summer in a Day.' Can you take a look and tell your partner what you notice about them?" I flipped to the sheet of chart paper where I had listed my possible claims.

1. In "All Summer in a Day," Ray Bradbury uses the sun to symbolize hope.
2. In "All Summer in a Day," Ray Bradbury uses symbolism, repetition, and descriptive language to show the children's need for freedom.

"Turn and talk, what do you see?" The class began discussing as I listened in. Within seconds I brought them back together. "Okay, so what I heard you saying is that in the first one, I focus on one craft move and a big idea about why the author seems to use it in the text. And in the second claim, I list a few craft moves the author uses—all for the same purpose. I'm going to sum this up in another bullet added to our chart."

How to Write an Author's Craft Essay

- Collect entries on the author's craft.

  - Choose a spot in the text to study and name a few craft moves you see the author using.

  - Look for patterns of craft across the text in similar scenes.

  - Focus on powerful craft moves, like symbolism.

- **Write a claim for author's craft, either focusing on one or many craft moves.**

"So you are ready, I think, to do this work—in a moment you will talk to your partner and try to draft a quick claim that follows one of these formats. Will you go with Option A, and focus on one craft move and a big idea that you have about it? Or will you try out Option B, and focus on a few craft moves your author used, that all work toward the same purpose? One thing you might take note of—see how if you focus on one craft move there'd better be lots of examples of it in the text? And how in the second option, all of the craft moves have to have the same purpose?" The class nodded. "Okay, try it out with your partner. See what claims you come up with."

Soon I brought the class back together.

"Oooh, I heard some pretty fascinating possibilities for claims. Danielle, can you share what you came up with?"

Danielle said, "Well, I'm working on *Divergent* and I realized that I had found a lot of stuff that I think is about, like, making us see things from Tris's perspective. So I came up with the claim, 'In *Divergent*, Veronica Roth uses inner thinking, descriptive language, and comparisons to make Tris's perspective clear.'"

SUPPORTING YOUR CLAIM

"Know that tomorrow, you'll be planning how your essay might go, and starting to draft, so having thought about and written down some possible claims will help a lot. Your planning and drafting will go much more smoothly if you've also thought about the reasons and evidence that you can use to support your claim. What you will want to consider doing tonight, after you have jotted down several possible claims, is to go back through the text as well as your writer's notebook entries to see what evidence you have at hand to support your claims.

"Take a moment and decide how you'll do that—will you read over all your entries and then write a new entry listing some possible claims? Will you continue collecting, marking possible claims in the margins? Will you go back to the text and use Post-it notes to mark places where you are finding evidence? Or will you go back through your writer's notebook, making similar annotations? When you've decided what you'll do, be sure to write that down. I can't wait to see what you've done tomorrow!"

Planning the Author's Craft Essay

Dear Teachers,

During this session you will be ushering your students to begin drafting their second essay of this unit—this time on the author's craft. By this point in their middle school careers, your students will have written many essays in many classes. So far with you they have already written one, so your hope may be that the bulk of your students are able to consider how to write an additional essay and will be able to take a stab at drafting one without so much support from you.

Your classes have worked with "boxes and bullets"—an elegant template designed to help students quickly draft an outline for their essays. They have learned to find supports, usually reasons, that their claim is true. They have also learned that when writing about texts, sometimes the structure follows an "in the beginning, in the middle, at the end" structure instead.

Now in this session you will show students several templates for planning a craft essay, reminding them that they may decide to focus on one craft move, showing how that one move is used in the beginning, middle, and end of a text, or they may show that an author uses a cluster of different craft moves to advance one idea. The latter structure is easier, as the essayists can draw on a wider array of observations. While there is no right answer, you will push your students to choose what they think the most powerful structure will be for their thinking about the text. This choice is central to this session and pushes your students to become more independent thinkers and writers.

In this session, however, we do offer students one helpful boost as they reach for this independence—a clear structural choice when considering exactly how a craft essay could go.

COMMON CORE STATE STANDARDS: W.8.1, W.8.4, W.8.5, W.8.9.a, W.8.10, RL.8.1, RL.8.2, RL.8.3, RL.8.4, SL.8.1, L.8.1, L.8.2, L.8.3

MINILESSON

To begin this lesson, you might want to highlight for students how often your lessons start with a metaphor—just like many of their favorite authors. You might remind them of a few memorable metaphors you have used to open lessons—often, a few sayings, metaphors, or stories stick with one class more than another and end up as miniature anchor experiences for that group of kids. Giving them an "insider's look" at your lessons can offer a more adult view on your work with them and your work together. When I taught this lesson recently, a student said, "Miss, I never knew you worked on that intro part, I thought you were just talking."

Then, let them know that a metaphor for the work you are going to do today—planning an author's craft essay—is that today's work entails making a choice about how you will spend your time that is very much like a choice they will be making next year in high school. Tell them that next year they will have to choose whether to devote their extracurricular time to one area—like theater—or if they will want to try out a whole bunch of activities—like theater, basketball, and math club. Point out that while either choice is great, one asks you to go deep with your study in a field, whereas the other allows you to sample more that life has to offer, but not as profoundly.

Then name the teaching point: That writers of author's craft essays pause and plan how their craft essays will go, and that when they do this they have to choose whether to focus in deeply on one craft move or whether to instead analyze a few they see in the text. Then, they start writing.

Next, you will want to show your students two ways that your essay could go. You will have premade these outlines for speed and efficiency. This lesson is not teaching students how to plan an essay as much as it is offering students a choice and asking them to make a smart one. Show your outlines, which may look something like these:

I. In "All Summer in a Day," Ray Bradbury uses the sun to symbolize hope.

- In the beginning the sun is shown as something the children dream of at night.
- In the middle the sun comes out and the children come to life.
- At the end when the sun goes away, the reality of their life and what they did hits them hard.
- Throughout, Bradbury uses figurative language to link the sun to warm, happy, hopeful things.

II. In "All Summer in a Day," Ray Bradbury uses symbolism, repetition, and descriptive language to show the children's need for freedom.

- He uses symbolism to express the children's need for freedom.
- He uses descriptive language to express the children's need for freedom.
- He uses repetition to express the children's need for freedom.

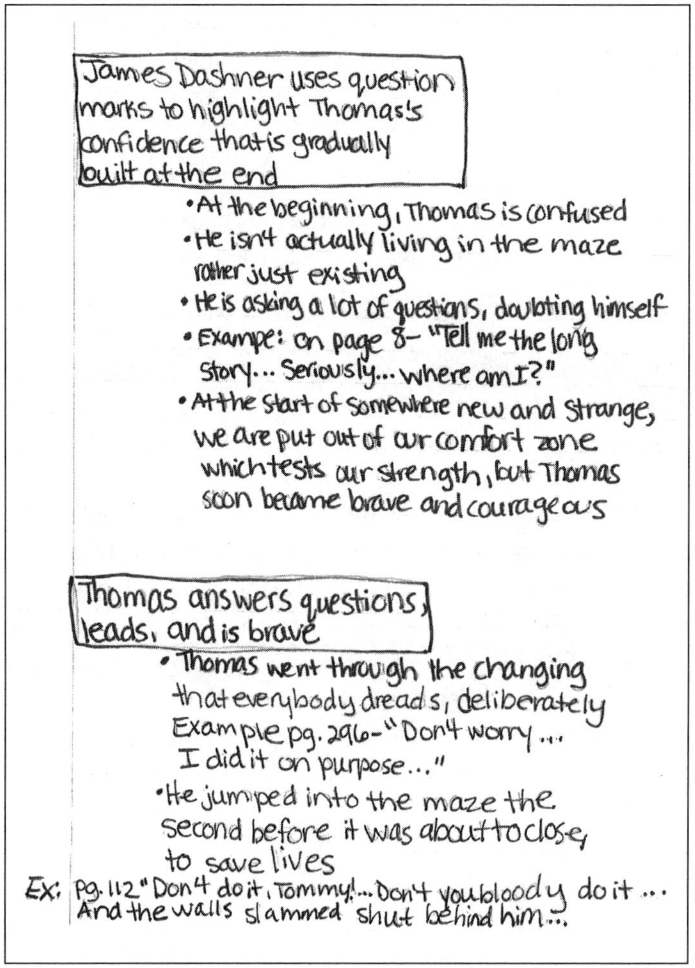
James Dashner uses question marks to highlight Thomas's confidence that is gradually built at the end

- At the beginning, Thomas is confused
- He isn't actually living in the maze rather just existing
- He is asking a lot of questions, doubting himself
- Example: on page 8– "Tell me the long story… Seriously… where am I?"
- At the start of somewhere new and strange, we are put out of our comfort zone which tests our strength, but Thomas soon became brave and courageous

Thomas answers questions, leads, and is brave

- Thomas went through the changing that everybody dreads, deliberately Example pg. 296– "Don't worry… I did it on purpose…"
- He jumped into the maze the second before it was about to close, to save lives

Ex: Pg. 112 "Don't do it, Tommy!… Don't you bloody do it… And the walls slammed shut behind him…

FIG. 11–1 Celine outlines two possible plans for her author's craft essay.

You may also choose to share with your students the more generalized frames of these essay outlines, minus the specifics that pertain to "All Summer in a Day":

I. Claim: (Author) focused deeply on (one craft move) . . . to . . . (purpose).

- In the beginning . . . the author uses . . . to (purpose).
- In the middle . . . the author uses . . . to (purpose).
- Throughout/at the end . . . the author uses . . . to (purpose).

II. Claim: (Author) focused on multiple craft moves . . . to . . . (purpose).

- The author uses craft move one . . . to . . . (purpose).
- The author uses craft move two . . . to . . . (purpose).
- The author uses craft move three . . . to . . . (purpose).

Show your students how the first example might be a good one for them if they feel like they can say a lot about one craft move—and if they see it repeating or growing across the text a bit. Point out how their work in this kind of essay is going to be focusing on how the author uses a signature craft move to illuminate a text's theme across a story. Then look at the difference in the second plan. You might have your class discuss a bit what makes the second plan different from the first—and what might be harder and easier about it. Kids have told me recently that the second one is easier in a way because you don't need to know quite as much about a particular craft move—you can select a few different things—but that it is also harder because you need to know and be able to talk about a bunch of craft moves, not just the one.

Of course there is no one right answer for how a writer knows which plan will work for them. If students are struggling to choose, you could coach them to use their notebooks to guide them—if students notice their notebook entries circling mostly around one main craft move, then the first may work best. The second structure will work best if their notebooks are an array of diverse observations about craft. In either case, have your students work with their partners to first select which plan they think will work best for them and then to rehearse how that plan will go for their particular essay. As you listen in, coach students to always be reaching for the why of these craft choices—what purpose the author may have had or what they were trying to show by writing like that.

As you bring the class together, canvass your students to see which plan they chose. Ask them to raise their hands if they chose one, then the other. Let them know that as they work today they can always switch over if their plan is not working, and advise them to pay attention to who in the class tried their plan the other way in case they need help.

Considering that some of their planning work is done during this lesson, most students will only need to take a bit of time to flesh out the rest of their plans, perhaps even trying out the other structure, just to see if it works better, before they start drafting. Of course, this is not your students' first essay rodeo. You will need to set them up for their work today in a way that leans on what they have already been taught about drafting essays. You may even want to directly lean on the "What Makes a Great Essay?" chart that was created in Session 4, when students began drafting their thematic essays. This is yet another way to promote transference, reminding students that an essay is an essay, and all that they have learned in the past about essay writing, whether it was a week or a year ago, should be brought forward. Before you send them off for writing workshop, ask students to think through what they will need to do to get ready to start their essays. Ask them to jot down in their notebook another quick To-Do list for their work, and focus their attention on the tools in the room that might help them.

Above all, let them know that you expect them to keep themselves working today (as every day), and that they should be using the classroom (charts, checklists, and partners) and their past teaching to help them do just that.

CONFERRING AND SMALL-GROUP WORK

On this day you will certainly have some students who struggle to get started after their first step of planning is done. As usual, instead of telling them what their next step is, encourage them to instead think about what tool or past teaching might help them to get themselves going. This work is critically important for your eighth-graders. For them, the ability to sustain their own work, to problem solve, to address their confusion, will make much of the difference in whether they thrive in high school, where in most cases they will receive less support. As an eighth-grade teacher you do not want to remove all support from underneath them, but you will want to be sure that the support you give encourages the development of independence. Coach your students to make a choice that they think will help them move forward, and then cheerlead their next steps.

You can also lean on the strong partnerships in your classroom. Just because you will not be there to help them as they get older does not mean they will be alone. Regardless of the independence expected of them in high school, they will always have classmates that can help keep them accountable and doing their best work. By encouraging these partnerships to thrive this year in eighth grade, you can set a foundation for how your students will work together in the years to come. This encouragement could mean reminding students of the ways their partners can be helpful to them as they work, conducting the occasional conference with a partnership rather than an individual writer, coaching them in how to best help one another, or reviewing systems you may have in place to support kids' partnership work, like places in the room where partners can work together.

Other conferring and small-group work you might expect to conduct includes supporting students whose planning doesn't quite work for them. In some cases, this might be because students chose a structure quickly, without regard to the type of claim they are making. For these students, you might coach them by asking questions to illuminate their options and reasoning, and point out that the types of questions you asked them are the questions that, really, they need to ask themselves in the future. In other cases, students might have made a reasonable decision but found themselves in trouble when they began drafting, perhaps having less to say about one craft move than they thought they did. These students may need a reminder that writers are willing to change directions when something isn't working. Though this was the focus of your teaching not long ago, it's daunting to do this as a writer, and kids may need your support if they are to change direction with confidence.

MID-WORKSHOP TEACHING

As students are working, be on the lookout for any students who are developing their own way of doing things so that you might use them as an example to the group. This might mean a way of outlining, a certain choice in steps they take, or kids who have decided to jump into drafting because they already know what they want to write.

Highlight what these students are doing as trendsetters in your classroom, and also highlight that students should look to each other as resources and peer teachers, always. Let students know that the most important thing is that they are making the smartest possible choices so their work will be the best it can possibly be. You might even mention that while you think your lessons are pretty outstanding, you know that one lesson will not work perfectly for every student, and that it is their responsibility to make sure their work makes sense to them before they just plow ahead.

SHARE

As students begin their essays, you might consider having them check in on their progress. Using a checklist like you did in the last bend will help with this self-assessment work; however, this time you will have to choose which checklist would most benefit your students. If, for example, you feel that they have pretty much mastered the seventh-grade checklist both last

Argument Writing Checklist

	Grade 7	NOT YET	STARTING TO	YES!	Grade 8	NOT YET	STARTING TO	YES!
	Structure				**Structure**			
Overall	I laid out a well-supported argument and made it clear that this argument is part of a bigger conversation about a topic/text. I acknowledged positions on the topic or text that might disagree with my own position, but I still showed why my position makes sense.	☐	☐	☐	I laid out an argument about a topic/text and made it clear why my particular argument is important and valid. I stayed fair to those who might disagree with me by describing how my position is one of several and making it clear where my position stands in relation to others.	☐	☐	☐
Lead	I interested the reader in my argument and helped them to understand the backstory behind it. I gave the backstory in a way that got the reader ready to see my point.	☐	☐	☐	After hooking the reader, I provided specific context for my own as well as another position(s), introduced my position, and oriented readers to the overall line of argument I planned to develop.	☐	☐	☐
	I made it clear to readers what my piece will argue and forecasted the parts of my argument.	☐	☐	☐				
Transitions	I used transitions to link the parts of my argument. The transitions help the reader follow from part to part and make it clear when I am stating a claim or counterclaim, giving a reason, or offering or analyzing evidence. These transitions include terms such as *as the text states, this means, another reason, some people may say, but, nevertheless,* and *on the other hand.*	☐	☐	☐	I used transitions to lead the reader across parts of the text and to help the reader note how parts of the text relate back to earlier parts. I used phrases such as *now some argue, while this may be true, it is also the case that, despite this, as stated earlier, taken as a whole, this is significant because, the evidence points to,* and *and by doing so . . .*	☐	☐	☐
Ending	In my conclusion, I reinforced and built on the main point(s) in a way that makes the entire text a cohesive whole. The conclusion may reiterate how the support for my claim outweighed the counterclaim(s), restate the main points, respond to them, or highlight their significance.	☐	☐	☐	In the conclusion, I described the significance of my argument for stakeholders, or offered additional insights, implications, questions, or challenges.	☐	☐	☐

year and in the last bend, then you might want to give them the eighth-grade list to use so that they may set some new goals. You may also decide to give them the two checklists side by side, so that they can see where they are, and where they need to push themselves to be. Of course, this is an opportunity for you to offer students different checklists depending on their level of comfort, and this will enable you and your students to work on different levels of goal-setting for the rest of this bend, if not the unit.

Have your students begin by naming (to themselves by annotating their writing, or to a partner who is working with them) what they have held on to from the last essay they wrote, and ask them to identify that work on the checklist or chart. Then push your class to broaden their view to at least one other row of the checklist—perhaps a category that best fits the writing they have done so far, or one that they have avoided thinking too much about until now. They will also want to refer to your classroom charts to help them set goals and assess their progress. Your anchor chart may now look something like this:

How to Write an Author's Craft Essay

- Collect entries on the author's craft.
  - Choose a spot in the text to study and name a few craft moves you see the author using.
  - Look for patterns of craft across the text in similar scenes.
  - Focus on powerful craft moves, like symbolism.
- Write a claim for author's craft, either focusing on one or many craft moves.
- **Plan how your essay will go and begin drafting.**

Like the last time your students wrote essays, encourage them to set doable goals for themselves for the next part of their essay, which you will encourage them to keep working on for homework that night.

Best,
Kate and Katy

Session 12

Framing Essays with Relevance and Context
Introductions and Conclusions

THIS SESSION FOCUSES on writing the introduction to an essay. As eighth-graders, your students will be expected to be able to not only introduce the text and claim of their essay, they will also be expected to write introductions that make the essay to come feel relevant. This entails reaching for the universal within the specifics of the text. It means acquiring the ability to step back from a story, a fact, or even an event in our lives and think, "How would this relate to everyone? What is the universal feeling, issue, or idea here?" This is a powerful ability indeed, and it is the heart of this session.

Showing kids how to find and highlight the universal relevance in their ideas can be a challenge, but one that will pay off for them even beyond the single introduction paragraph. Searching for universality will help your students deepen their understanding of why authors write stories and why other writers spend time writing about those stories. Building context, too, can be tricky, as your kids will tend to bubble over with plot, setting, and character information about their texts that feels crucial to share with readers. Before you—or they—know it, they have a lengthy recounting of their stories rather than a tight, thoughtful introductory paragraph.

You will model the steps kids will need to take to think about finding the relevance in their ideas and then to express that clearly to their readers. You'll then demonstrate writing just a sentence or two giving the context of the story for readers, angled to reflect the ideas that the essay will be highlighting. Finally, you'll ask students to try this work with their own introductions, with the support of a partner.

As students work today, and you coach and confer, you'll support kids in revising their work in many ways, trying to coach them to draw on a whole repertoire of skills. Finally, at the end of the session you will channel the class to think about what they already know about conclusions, to work on the endings to their essays. Throughout the day, you'll help students draw on all their resources so that they come in the next day with a complete draft, ready to dive headfirst into the work of revision.

IN THIS SESSION, you'll teach students that essayists write introductions that explain the text being analyzed and the greater relevance of their essays. They often conclude their essays by leaving readers with their most powerful thoughts.

GETTING READY

- ✔ Chart paper and markers (see Teaching and Share)

- ✔ Students' essay drafts (see Active Engagement)

- ✔ "How to Write an Author's Craft Essay" anchor chart (see Link and Homework)

- ✔ "How to Write a Thematic Essay" chart (see Link and Conferring and Small-Group Work)

- ✔ "Narrative Writers Aim Toward Goals Such As . . ." chart (see Conferring and Small-Group Work)

- ✔ Your own essay conclusion, enlarged for students to see (see Share)

COMMON CORE STATE STANDARDS: W.8.1.a,e; W.8.3.b, W.8.9.a, RI.8.1, RL.8.1, RL.8.2, RL.8.4, SL.8.1, SL.8.4, L.8.1, L.8.2, L.8.3

Framing Essays with Relevance and Context

Introductions and Conclusions

CONNECTION

Name a time that you were introduced to something without relevance or context. Link this experience to reading an essay with a weak introduction.

"Once, when I was about nine or ten, I came home from school and my mom was in the kitchen with a kid I didn't know—a sad-looking boy. As soon as I walked in the door Mom said, 'Hi honey, this is your cousin Mark. He will be staying with us a while.' It took me so much by surprise that I didn't act that great—I think I rolled my eyes and probably looked really unhappy and weird.

"Later my mom explained things to me—that I had never met him because his parents had problems and Mom hadn't wanted me around them, that Mark needed a place to stay and people to love him, and that family was important, being generous was important, and she wanted me to try and be more like a generous family member in the future.

"I felt so embarrassed for how I had acted that day with Mark—rolling my eyes and stuff—and what I told my mom was, 'You know, it would have helped if I'd known all this!'

"Being introduced to things is important—especially when it's not obvious how something relates to you or why it matters. This is true in life, and it is certainly true in literary essays. When you are writing essays about an author's craft, it is especially important to start off your essay making sure your reader knows why this topic is relevant, as well as the context of the story."

❖ **Name the teaching point.**

"So today I want to teach you that essayists introduce their essays by explaining the context of the text and also by naming how the ideas in the essay might be relevant to the reader."

This story works on so many levels. First, it helps create a personal connection between you and your students, which builds trust and positive relations with your adolescent charges. On another level, this anecdote clearly illustrates the importance of context and background information in a real-life setting, which you will then go on to connect to students' writing lives.

TEACHING

Demonstrate finding some universal relevance in your own essay topic.

"Let me show you what I mean in my essay, with my introduction. I want to make sure my introduction explains a bit about this story and gives an idea of its relevance to the reader, so my readers don't start off confused, the way I was with my cousin Mark. It's almost as if my introduction has three distinct parts to it: part one—providing relevance to my reader through naming the universality of my idea; part two—providing the context by summarizing the text just a little bit; and part three—stating my claim clearly.

"I will start with the relevance bit. When I am reaching for the relevance in an essay, I have to think a bit about why anyone else would care about this essay, this claim. My essay is about how in 'All Summer in a Day,' Ray Bradbury uses the sun to symbolize hope. Take a second and think about that. What part of my claim could other people relate to? Give me a thumbs up if you have an idea." I waited a moment until a collection of thumbs were in the air. "Lucas?"

Lucas said, "Well, everyone relates to hope."

"Right! Okay, so I could start off my essay then like this." I turned to a fresh sheet of chart paper, and began a possible essay introduction:

> Everyone in life needs to believe that things are going to get better, especially when facing tough times.

Move on to model how you also include context in your introductions.

"Now let's work on the context. Just like I needed my mom to tell me what was going on with my cousin, in essays we need to tell our readers a little something about the story. Usually that looks like a line or two that summarizes a bit of the text. But here is the thing—our summary should still stay relevant to the topic of the essay. I need to summarize the story through the lens of the idea I kicked things off with—in this case, hope. And I'm going to need to try and keep it to a sentence or two tops; otherwise things get really bulky. I'm going to try that out here."

I spoke as I continued to write in front of the class. "So first I have 'Everyone in life needs to believe that things are going to get better, especially when facing tough times.' Now I want to summarize this story through the lens of hardship. So I could write 'In "All Summer in a Day," by Ray Bradbury, the characters have a tough life. Unending rain. Gray skies and cold. The same thing day after day. But when the children are asleep at night, they hope for more. When the children sleep, they dream of the sun.'" I recorded the next portion of my introduction.

Finish your introduction by writing your claim clearly.

"Okay, so I think I have a good sense of relevance, and I have set up a little context. Now, for the claim. I know I don't have to tell you that it's important in your introductions to state your claim, usually in the last line. So now my introduction will look like this . . ." I finished writing in front of the class:

While it may appear that you are crafting your introduction on the fly and with the help of your students, you will have indeed thought through this paragraph before you began the minilesson. You don't need to have the entire introduction crafted, just some ideas for the various parts of it (explaining the context of the text as well as the universality of your ideas). You do want to record the introduction, rather than simply write-in-the-air. That way, your students will have some artifact to refer back to when they begin to craft their own introductory paragraphs.

Because your students have written introductions before, this lesson is designed to be a fast-paced model of how one introduction was written. If you find that your class needs more support, take more time here to explain exactly how you came to each part of your introduction.

Everyone in life needs to believe that things are going to get better, especially when facing tough times. In "All Summer in a Day," by Ray Bradbury, the characters have a tough life. Unending rain. Gray skies and cold. The same thing day after day. But when the children are asleep at night, they hope for more. When the children sleep, they dream of the sun. In "All Summer in a Day," Bradbury uses the sun throughout the story to symbolize hope.

Debrief the steps you took.

"Okay, so when I want to make sure my introductions have relevance and context, I first think about what is universal in my thinking and write a line or two about that idea. Then I summarize the text a bit through the lens of that universal idea, and lastly I make sure to state my claim clearly at the end of my introduction."

ACTIVE ENGAGEMENT

Usher students to practice their introductions with a partner.

"So right now, work with your partner to see how one of your introductions can go—say it aloud, exactly how it might sound. Partners, we will only have time to practice one introduction right now, so be sure to choose which of you either needs the most help or has the longest To-Do list. Okay, get started."

As the class worked together I moved around the room coaching pairs that seemed stuck, saying things like, "To help you find the universal, focus on a word in your claim that you think people would relate to—like I did with *hope*," or "Sometimes you need to try out your summary a few times to get it right. Don't be afraid to redo it."

After a moment, I said, "Nice work everyone. One thing I noticed is how you had to try out what you wanted to say a few times. That might be something you will need to do in writing today, too. Remember, you can always practice a few introductions in your notebooks before you choose one for your draft."

LINK

Make sure that students know the range of their work for the day.

"Of course, you will not just be writing introductions today. Many of you are in different places with your essays. Will you just talk to your partner quickly to say what it is you will be working on during writing workshop today? I will show you our anchor chart so far for this essay, but remember to use any of the charts in the room. It might help you, for example, to look at our 'How to Write a Thematic Essay' chart as well to see what work you might need to take on today."

I gave the class about ten seconds to talk and then brought them back together. "Great. Off you go."

Of course, you may be thinking, there are other ways to start a literary essay! You're correct, of course. Another way this session could have gone would be to lay out some possibilities and encourage students to try different introductions on for size. I chose to teach in this way because the challenge of providing context for the reader without overdoing the plot summary, and while still reaching for relevance, can be daunting. This introduction helps students tackle both challenges head-on.

Don't be concerned if some students mimic your sentence construction—copying the style of a mentor is one of the best ways to learn to write. Encouraging students to look at a mentor text is a way to provide scaffolding for them without falling into the trap of giving suggestions like "Don't you think hope is universal?"

The language you use in your link is all-important; it can determine whether students remember your lesson as "today's assignment" or as a strategy they will draw upon when it's needed. Though of course all the students will need to write introductions soon, I deliberately spoke in a way that reminded students of their larger purpose and their responsibility to make writerly choices.

How to Write an Author's Craft Essay

- Collect entries on the author's craft.
  - Choose a spot in the text to study and name a few craft moves you see the author using.
  - Look for patterns of craft across the text in similar scenes.
  - Focus on powerful craft moves, like symbolism.
- Write a claim for author's craft, either focusing on one or many craft moves.
- Plan how your essay will go and begin drafting.
- **Write introductions that summarize the story, explain the essay's relevance, and state the claim.**

How to Write a Thematic Essay

- Collect ideas about the themes in a text.
  - Name a central problem or issue that characters in the story face.
  - Reflect on parts of the story that pertain to this problem.
  - Think to yourself, "What is this story teaching me about this problem, this issue?"
  - Write long about your thinking to grow your ideas, perhaps by asking how different characters relate to that issue.
- Go back to the text and reread closely to see how the theme works in certain critical scenes.
- Look for purposeful craft moves the author used and think about how they reveal more about the theme.
- Write a claim and a plan for your essay and use a mentor text to begin drafting.
- Search for places where your writing isn't working and do what's necessary to fix it.
- Logically explain how your evidence supports your thinking about the text.
- Add writing that addresses alternative ideas to yours, being sure to show how your thinking is better.

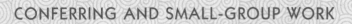

Working to Get It "Right"

ALTHOUGH YOUR STUDENTS will indeed have many different tasks on their agendas for this day of writing, you will probably find that many of them tackle the work of introductions right off the bat. Although you have provided them with a strong, straightforward strategy, you will probably have a group of students who are eager to try something different. For these students, you might teach a way of introducing essays that has a little more voice, a bit more spirit. Teach them that essayists sometimes start with a powerful, brief moment from the text, angling that moment to fit the topic or claim of the essay, and then gracefully transitioning from the moment into the larger context and claim. You will want to model this strategy for this group of writers, perhaps with an introduction like this one:

> At the very end of Ray Bradbury's "All Summer in a Day," the rocket children have played in the sun for the first time in seven years. Then, after only two hours, they feel the first drop of the endless rain returning and instantly, all the dullness and hardship of living in a world with no sun comes rushing back. They hurry inside to escape the storm and suddenly remember that there will be seven more years of the same rain, the same gray skies. They also must face what they have done to poor, grieving Margot—the girl they locked in a closet out of jealousy and meanness so that she would miss the sun's appearance. Venus is a planet of grueling hardship, and Ray Bradbury uses repetition throughout this short story to emphasize the hardships the characters face.

On the other hand, you might also encounter students who, despite your modeling, are having a hard time trying out an introduction. Sometimes the beginning of a piece can feel paralyzing, even when a student has a good chunk of the body written. These students could benefit from a few practice attempts. You could coach this group to try several versions of the introduction—perhaps writing out three different summaries of the text, or three different statements about the essay's relevance—to help break the ice. Even if all three end up being somewhat similar, the thought that each is just one choice out of many can be freeing to students who are hesitant.

You're also likely to confer today with some writers who seem ready to connect the craft they've noticed to its purpose, or even the themes of the text, but aren't quite there yet. You might notice these students writing well about craft, but stumbling when it comes to the bigger idea or purpose behind the craft. I noticed Rachel struggling with this problem and coached her to use the "Narrative Writers Aim Toward Goals Such As" chart from Session 9 first to come up with some of the effects that the

MID-WORKSHOP TEACHING
Reminding Students to Draw on All Their Resources

"Writers, let me stop you for a moment. I see you all working hard—great job! Something to remember about how writers work is that they often turn to resources around them to help out. What resources can you all remember to use as you work on this essay? Brainstorm with your partner for a minute.

"I heard some people mentioning charts, earlier parts of their writing notebooks, their partners . . . I bet there were more ideas I didn't hear, too.

"What made me think of this was a conference I just had with Flynn. We were talking about Flynn's next steps. He's written a pretty solid introduction, and he felt like he needed to revise some of his body paragraphs. He thought that maybe he could get some good ideas for what to improve by looking at the Argument Writing Checklist, so he went to get that. How great is that? Instead of just waiting for someone else, like me, to tell him what he can do to get better, he remembered, on his own, a resource that he had. So don't forget as you continue to write—you have resources to draw on, and part of being strong as a writer is knowing how and when to use them."

techniques she found might be having on the reader. Rachel had already noticed many short sentences and the author's use of dashes, and with some urging to look at the "Narrative Writers Aim Toward Goals Such As . . ." chart, she said that she thought the author may have written like that to build a mood and also to build suspense. I then asked Rachel if she could think across the whole unit so far, looking for some strategies that might help her to explain how the craft she noticed in the text achieved the purpose she had identified. As Rachel thought, I pointed toward the "How to Write a Thematic Essay" chart from the first bend of the unit.

"Oh!" Rachel said. "Right, I forgot we did all of that stuff about explaining—using the thought prompts and even thinking about the logic behind what we were saying."

I asked if she thought she could try out some of these past strategies on her new essay, and she nodded vigorously.

In each case, you are pushing your students to step away from their drafts, working on a part of their essay until they get it "right." This is an invaluable lesson. As you teach your students to write, helping them to stop when they are having trouble and making sure they work to solve the inevitable problems that arise could be a lesson that will stay with them for years to come.

Narrative Writers Aim Toward Goals Such As...

Provide the context/background information	Introduce the characters	Show the character's motivation
Stir empathy	Create the setting	Build a mood
Set up the problem	Raise the stakes	Build suspense
Get readers predicting	Support the theme	Show the resolution

He vomits.

In this quote, Patrick Ness cuts many sentences short and suddenly stops in the middle of a huge concept. The reason for this is to make the reader think, What exactly is going on? This also shows that the protagonist, in this case, Seth, was trying to piece together bits of information with the reader. Patrick Ness has a unique style of writing and that is what gets the reader hooked on his books. Ness uses short sentences in order to show that the protagonist is trying to piece together the world around him. For example, in the previous quote on page 20, Seth is beginning to piece together bits of his life, he is just starting to figure out the truth, but when Seth is on the verge of getting some answers, the sentence stops. This shows how abrupt his life really

FIG. 12–1   Rachel's developing essay benefits from some time spent reflecting on techniques she'd learned earlier.

Crafting Powerful Conclusions

Push students to recall what they already know about writing conclusions.

"It's pretty clear how hard you were all working today. Many of you, in fact, have a pretty solid draft going, and you'll be ready to finish that draft for homework tonight. The one part we haven't talked so much about is your conclusion—not because it doesn't matter, but because you already know quite a bit about conclusions! You know that as an essayist, it's important that you leave your reader with some of your most powerful thoughts. With your partner, list out some strategies you already know for writing powerful conclusions."

I circulated between partnerships, listening in and jotting students' ideas on my clipboard. I then reconvened the class. "Impressive! You all remembered quite a bit about ways to close your essay. Let's jot down a little of what you said." I listed students' ideas about conclusions on a sheet of chart paper.

Great Conclusions Might . . .

- Restate the claim, finding another way to say the same thing.
- Leave readers with something to think about.
- Show how the claim of the essay connects to your own life or may connect to the lives of your readers.
- Suggest a further way of acting, or of thinking.
- Show how your thinking about the claim changed as you reread.

"Writers, think about your particular essays now, and make a plan for what you'll do to make sure you end your essays strong. One thing that often helps is to try your conclusion a couple of different ways, to see which works best. You might think about trying that. Another thing that can be really helpful is to study a mentor text—so I put one possible conclusion I'm considering for my essay up on chart paper for you take a look at."

In "All Summer in a Day," the sun symbolizes the hope that lives in the human heart. The hope for something better, the hope that things will change. The sun in "All Summer in a Day" is warm, it lights up the world, but it also leaves. At the end of the story the reader is left to wonder–are the children better off for having experienced the warmth of the sun's rays? Are they better off for experiencing such hope? While we leave the story seeing how powerful hope can be, we are also left wondering if hope is really worth it in the end.

FINISHING YOUR DRAFT

"So tonight, you will finish your draft! Look over your work and make a quick plan for what specifically you'll need to do to accomplish this. Don't forget to use any charts and checklists that might help you. Here is our chart for writing an author's craft essay, which can be a great resource."

How to Write an Author's Craft Essay

- Collect entries on the author's craft.
  - Choose a spot in the text to study and name a few craft moves you see the author using.
  - Look for patterns of craft across the text in similar scenes.
  - Focus on powerful craft moves, like symbolism.
- Write a claim for author's craft, either focusing on one or many craft moves.
- Plan how your essay will go and begin drafting.
- Write introductions that summarize the story, explain the essay's relevance, state the claim, **and write strong conclusions.**

"Write those tasks down someplace so you remember to do them! You are in the home stretch, so this is a time to keep up the energy you've shown today—don't let your focus drop now! If you are a little worried about what you need to do tonight to finish, be sure to let me know after class so we can talk it through."

Adopting an Essayist's Tone

IN THIS SESSION, you'll teach students that writers can adopt an essayist's engaging and formal tone by varying their sentence length and using sophisticated language.

GETTING READY

✔ Chart paper and markers (see Connection and Link)

✔ An excerpt from a former student's essay that can be used to revise for tone, enlarged for students to see (see Teaching)

✔ Students' essay drafts and pens (see Active Engagement and Share)

COMMON CORE STATE STANDARDS: W.8.1.a,b,c,d,e; W.8.3.b,d; W.8.5, W.8.9.a, RL.8.4, SL.8.1, L.8.1, L.8.2, L.8.3, L.8.6

116

AS ADULTS, we know that sometimes tone is everything. The right tone can win a job or earn forgiveness from a friend; the wrong tone can cause a big fight at home. In essay writing, the Common Core State Standards also call for middle school students to work with tone, expecting them to use it to "establish and maintain a formal style" in their information writing. In this session, you'll help your students grapple with tone to make their essays become more formal without losing a sense of voice. In the course of this session, you will likely find that by striving for an essayist's tone, voice in their pieces actually flourishes rather than flees!

Your teaching in this session will invite students to use word choice and sentence length to experiment with tone in their writing. They will also revise in general, based on all they know, and you will end the session by providing them with an opportunity to notice and celebrate the effects of their thoughtful revision. Ideally, students will be eager to jump in and try playing with sentence length, substituting different words, and rereading to hear the effect of their choices. Do everything you can to encourage a sense of experimentation and trying new things—the seriousness of this topic, steeped in Common Core Standards and formality, doesn't mean the end of joy in our classrooms.

As students begin working, you will encourage them to not just revise for tone, but to revise using all they know about good essay writing. As they do this, you will be assessing how well your class is holding onto the lessons of this unit. Are they remembering to clarify the relationship between their evidence and ideas? Have they forgotten to mention alternative arguments? Certainly you will want to be sure that they remember to add specific evidence, often in the form of quotes, as they write. Your list of "must-haves" might be different, but regardless of the specifics this will be a powerful time for you to get a sense of how sticky your teaching is, how deeply your students are learning what you offer them. In this session you will have the opportunity to remind students that it is their responsibility not to just take on the lesson of the day, but to carry with them the legacy of this unit—and of their school career.

Adopting an Essayist's Tone

CONNECTION

Set up the work for the day by introducing the idea of tone in essay writing.

"You all have your drafts out here in the meeting area?" Nods. "Everyone have a pen?" More nods. "Today we are going to be looking at the tone of our writing, and we are going to look for ways to adopt the most effective and engaging tone we can. Tone can be a tricky thing to pin down as a writer. But we all know it when we hear it. I am willing to bet that you speak in many tones across the day—to your friends, your frenemies, your teachers."

Have a student act out different tones for the class to study.

"Just imagine walking up to someone and saying hello to them. Now imagine if it's your best friend—Lauren, will you act that out with me for a second?" Lauren shrugged. "Great. So if you were starting a conversation with your best friend, what would you say? Exaggerate a little to help me make this point . . ."

Lauren smiled. "I would say, 'Hey! Oh my god how *are* you? How was last night?"

The class laughed. "Nice, Lauren. Okay. Now what if you were talking to someone you couldn't really stand but had to be polite to?"

Lauren sniffed. "Hello," she said with her lips pursed.

I laughed with the class. "Brilliant! So of course we know what different tones sound like, but can you all now talk to your partner—what did Lauren do to change the tone of her greeting? What did she do with her words, specifically? Discuss."

Listen in as students discuss. Point out that changes in sentence length, literary devices, and word choice affect the tone of the speaker.

I listened in and wrote down what the students noticed, namely that Lauren used short, clipped sentences when she didn't like the person, and that she used more casual language—even slang—when talking to a friend. I quickly scrawled my list on a sheet of chart paper and brought the class together. "So, what you all noticed today is what we

The nods from students, indicating they all have their materials, reflect work put in all year long to establish classroom routines to support writing workshop, like what materials to have ready. In middle school, your classroom time is precious; if you have to wait for students, or find they're frequently unprepared, you might want to engage your students in a problem-solving conversation.

This connection reinforces the work students have done with craft in this unit and others in middle school—they are, in their conversations, analyzing how a speaker creates an effect using craft.

are going to work on in our writing. That by changing things like the words we use, and the length of our sentences, we affect the tone of our writing."

❖ Name the teaching point.

"Today I am going to teach you that when essayists revise, they work to adopt an engaging and formal tone in their writing by varying their sentence length and making sure their language is sophisticated."

TEACHING

Channel students to try revising a former student's essay to give it more of an essayist's tone.

"So we are going to try this together on an essay that belongs to a former student of mine—working to see how we can give it more of an essayist's tone. In general, an essay should have a sort of formal, fancy tone, but it should also be interesting to read and kind of persuasive. You'll notice that this is not the case with the essay I have here. So let's read this part of my former student's essay and see if we can do some work with the word choice and sentence length to give it a formal, but engaging tone. Check this paragraph out, and see if you can find the places that don't feel very formal, or fancy, or even that interesting."

> In the middle, Thurber uses gloves to symbolize how trapped Walter is all the time. Walter does not want to be safe and warm. He wants to have adventures and be like a hero. But his wife keeps telling him to wear his gloves. Thurber uses this everyday thing to symbolize how Walter wants to get out.

"To revise this paragraph, I am going to ask you to think about two different things. First, let's try looking at the word choice. I can't help but notice that there is not much that is formal or engaging about the language here. Which words do you think you could revise to make more sophisticated or more interesting? Remember to think about the fancier ways you might talk about books when you do this."

Students started talking. I listened in. Some noticed that instead of saying "in the middle of the story," the writer could say, "Furthermore," or even nothing at all. Others picked up on words like "trapped" and "does not want" and changed them to more precise language like "suffocated," "rejects the safety and warmth of his life." I wrote these on the draft of the paragraph and brought the class together.

Model another way writers work on the tone of their essays—by varying the length of their sentences.

"Nice. It's sounding more 'essay-ish' already. So another way that you might work on the tone of an essay is to focus on the length of your sentences. One way writers do this is to combine sentences for more flow. They also will write short, emphatic sentences to really drive their point home. If I look at this part of the essay, I think I could combine these two sentences" (I pointed to the second and the third) "to say, 'Walter rejects the safety and warmth of his life—he wants to be the hero of his own adventures.'

Using a former student's work as your model is a powerful move—your students will be more interested in another kid's work, and it allows you to show revision before and after.

While the examples in this lesson are examples from students across the country, they may not match the level of your students, in your class-room, this year. Do not let this bother you. The point of this lesson is to make the writing more formal, more sophisticated—how much so will depend on the individuals in front of you.

"Can you look across the rest of this paragraph and see if there is anything else you could do with the sentences, either by combining them or writing a short, emphatic one?" After a moment of working together I asked Alec to share what he said to his partner.

"Um. I said maybe you could write after the hero sentence, 'But he isn't the hero of anything. He is just Walter.'"

"Oh look at you, Alec!" I beamed. "Two short sentences in a row. That *does* add sophistication to the tone."

I brought the class together. "So I acted on your suggestions. Let's look at our paragraph now and see if it feels more formal and engaging."

> Furthermore, Thurber uses gloves to symbolize how suffocated Walter is in the story. Walter rejects the safety and warmth of his life—he wants to be the hero of his own adventures. But he isn't the hero of anything. He is just Walter. Walter, whose wife keeps telling him to wear his gloves. Thurber uses this everyday object to symbolize how Walter wants to escape his life.

Debrief the steps you took.

"I've got chills. That is so good now! Okay, so what we did—we looked for words and phrases we could make more precise, sophisticated, and engaging, and then we tried to either combine some sentences or add some short emphatic ones."

ACTIVE ENGAGEMENT

Channel students to revise one of their paragraphs, working to give it a more formal and engaging tone.

"I think you are ready to try this in your own writing. And I think today you should try this on your own, here in the meeting area, for a minute, and then you can show your partner what you revised. So go ahead, and try some of this work we did today."

As students wrote, I looked for writers who seemed stuck, being sure to give them a gentle nudge first by saying things like, "Why don't you start by circling a couple words you think could be more precise?" When students struggled for a longer time, I made a note for my conferring work that day.

After a minute I asked the class to share with their partner what they tried. Jared was sharing his work with Flynn, saying, "So I basically changed like every word. I kept using the word 'think' in my original, so I tried to find other ways to say that. What did you do?" Flynn shrugged. "I kind of did the same thing—but then I saw a couple sentences I could combine, too."

Having students revise a piece of writing collectively allows them to try out a strategy and to see its impact without worrying about whether their own writing is up to snuff.

Though you'll certainly coach individual students during active engagements, be sure not to get so embroiled in a conversation with a single student that you're missing the bigger picture—the active engagement is your best opportunity in the lesson to get a read on how all your students are interpreting your teaching, and who is likely to be tackling which problems today. And, as I do here, this is a chance to do some purposeful planning for your conferring for the day.

I nodded. "Any start is good. You will have time to keep looking for places to revise for tone—today, tomorrow, and for the rest of your writing lives."

LINK

Add this strategy to your writer's repertoire for revising essays.

"So today all but a few of you are revising your essays. I know you know a bunch about revising, from our work together this year but also from all of your middle school years. Can you get together a bit and name a few things you know are important to do when you revise in general, and maybe a few things you would do in an essay?" I had the class discuss this in partners, and then I started a chart using what students named:

Eighth-Grade Guide to Revising

- Reread, looking for gaps in your piece.
- If you aren't sure if something makes sense, read it aloud or talk to a partner.
- Use your tools—checklists, charts, mentors.
- Pay attention to the language you use.
- Look at the transition language you use to guide your reader from part to part.
- Ask yourself how clear your evidence is and whether it completely supports your claim.
- Be aware of tone by thinking about word choice and sentence length.

"So today when you are working, you may want to work on your essay's tone, but be sure to remember all of the other work you might do to make your essays the best they can possibly be."

Although I could have listed these revision tips for the students, by having the class construct the chart themselves I am able to assess how well students are holding on to what I have taught them. If they had not been able to make anything when asked, I would have directed them to use the charts in the room, their partners, and their drafts to jog their memory.

Options for Your Students, and Your Coaching

MUCH OF YOUR SMALL-GROUP AND CONFERRING WORK today will probably center around helping students see alternatives and possibilities in their work. Here are a few of the tips and suggestions you may find yourself giving in conferences, small groups, and voiceovers to the class today:

◆ Some students who are tackling your invitation to look at *word choice* may find this challenging work. They may be able to pinpoint words that could be more sophisticated, but struggle to find better choices. Students may reach for a thesaurus in this situation, but this will often create even more cringe-worthy sentences as they arbitrarily select synonyms without knowledge of the words' connotations or shades of meaning. As an alternative, you could teach students to use mentor texts as an academic vocabulary resource. The model essay you've used in this unit, as well as many texts in the classroom, could be mined for more sophisticated transitions and turns of phrase that your students could adopt. It would be worthwhile to carry one of these texts with you as you confer today.

◆ You are likely to also have students who struggle to see possibilities for *revision* in their writing, who perhaps change a few words here, combine a few sentences there, and call it a day. For many students, a helpful coaching move is to remind them to revise with different lenses. You demonstrated this in your minilesson, after all—you were revising specifically for tone. You might coach these students to name some of the revision lenses that have been productive for them in the past—like elaboration, transitions, or clarity—and encourage them to select one and try revising with that individual lens. This would be a welcome alternative to rereading the text over and over, hoping for inspiration to strike.

◆ Sometimes students, despite your best efforts, will not be taking *lifelong writing skills* from your lessons; they will see revising for tone as the only work of the day. This might be because they are, for whatever reason, in an "assignment" mentality rather than the mind-set of a writer engaged in ongoing work. If you are noticing this frequently at this point, it will be worth reflecting on how your

(continues)

MID-WORKSHOP TEACHING   **Pushing Writers to Prioritize**

"Writers, hold on a moment. How many of you have revised some or most of your essay for tone today?" Almost every hand shot up in the air. "Okay, how many of you have revised for something else?" Only a few hands appeared. I nodded solemnly. "I am so proud of the work you are doing, but I do have to push you now—your job as essayists today is to revise your essays for the *most important* issues you see that need revision. That is the point, not just to follow my lesson blindly. So let me ask you a question—how many of you feel like tone is just the most absolutely important thing for you to spend the whole day on?" Again, only a few hands went up.

"I don't mean to sound stern, but really it is essential that you remember to prioritize what your work should be. Right now, talk to someone near you—if you were to revise for the most important thing in your essays, what would it be?" The students began to talk, and I listened in. After seconds I brought them together.

"So almost all of you have a different priority than what you were working on today. I am so glad you wanted to work on today's lesson, but from now on I expect you to be more strategic—always revise for the most important thing first, unless a teacher expressly tells you to spend all of your time doing something specific. Okay?" The class nodded.

BEFORE

In the book Harry Potter and the Sorcerer's Stone I notice a couple of patterns with theme and Personafacation. I saw Personifacation when children were being drafted to teams in Hogwarts. A Hat was talking and reading the childs brain. I also saw this when Professor mconagal was a cat and she started talking. Another Pattern was the theme Good vs. Evil showing up a lot. when Voldemort and Profesor cruel the evil guys tried to extermanate Harry and redeem the Sorcerers stone.

AFTER

In the book Harry Potter And The Sorcerers Stone I observed a couple of patterns with theme and personifacation. I discovered some Personifacation when children were being drafted to teams in Hogwarts. A hat was digging out childrens brains to place them on a team. I also encountered personifacation when Profesor MCgonagol was a cat and she started talking. Another pattern was when the the Good vs. Evil was poping up a lot. When voldemort and Profesor cruel the evil and cruel guys tried to exterminate Harry and redeem the sorcerers stone. Good vs. Evil was also shown when Harry was in the Quidditch match and voldemort and profesor cruel tried to cast a spell on Harrys broom. I think the author does these patems in the book because she wants to make it more infresting and more catchy. This kinda worked on me.

FIG. 13–1   Aren considers word choice in his essay.

teaching may be setting students up to see their work this way. For instance, do students have enough time to write? If not, it may be that they are only able to accomplish the work you laid out in the minilesson, rather than being pushed to draw on their repertoire of skills. If this is the case, you will want to adjust your teaching to avoid having to tackle the "I'm done" conversation over and over again.

Sharing Our Success

Channel students to see the impact of their revision work.

"Writers, today you might have felt a little like a contestant on one of those home makeover shows, turning your writing from casual to elegant. So in that spirit, let's take some time to really honor your work with the Extreme Makeovers: Essay Edition! Everyone, quick, take a moment to find your best chunk of revision today—a place where you really feel you nailed it! I'll give you just a moment to look for a place like this, and when you find it, put a star by that chunk in your draft."

After a minute, I said, "Okay, grab your partner and find another pair, get together into a group of four and share your Extreme Makeover sentences! Drumrolls are definitely encouraged!" The class burst into activity.

SESSION 13 HOMEWORK

WORKING EVEN HARDER

"Alright! That was pretty stunning, seeing all that you accomplished today. Which is perfect, because that means you are all set up for tonight's homework—to work even harder! I'm only sort of kidding. You got a lot done in class, but you'll want to get just as much done tonight to make your essays as phenomenal as they can be. Take a quick look at the chart we made today listing some of the revision work you know how to do, think about your essay, and write down at least three specific revision To-Do's that you'll get done tonight."

A Comma Inquiry

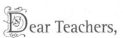ear Teachers,

This session is devoted to teaching your students powerful ways to construct their sentences, to work on their syntax, and to support and nurture their developing grammar. In this case, by learning multiple ways to use commas. Of course, you may choose to use this time to focus on another aspect of editing work needed more urgently by your students. After all, a top-down approach to conventions (relying on an outside source to determine what your conventions lessons should be) is relatively ineffective in the scheme of things. Most educators believe firmly that only by meeting your students where they are in their conventions work, and helping them grow from there, will you be able to find results.

While you will spend some time today teaching a whole-class lesson, you will do less "watch me use commas powerfully" (less demonstration) and more allowing students the opportunity to study the subject of commas themselves (more inquiry). In this lesson, you will set students up to do a quick, guided inquiry around why authors use commas, and then help them to find language for the varying ways that commas can make writing better. Then you will push your class to try out some of these moves in their own writing, ending your day with a reflection on editing in general and setting some goals for what editing work your students may focus on for the future.

MINILESSON

For your connection today, find an example of something in your life that you are careless with. Perhaps it is doing the nightly dishes, or the laundry. Or perhaps you are forgetful about birthdays. Whatever you choose, explain to your class how in these instances, even though you sort of know how to, say, wash the dishes, because you are careless, you are not very good at doing them—they wind up always seeming a little greasy, for example. Then story-tell about a time when you watched someone else wash the dishes, using really

COMMON CORE STATE STANDARDS: W.8.1, W.8.5, RL.8.10, SL.8.1, L.8.1, L.8.2.b, L.8.3

hot water and more soap than you usually do, and that these details, these *particular* ways of washing the dishes, helped you to be less careless and more proficient as a dishwasher.

You might say something along the lines of "Today I'm going to teach you that one way writers craft more powerful sentences is by paying attention to conventions, especially conventions that they might be careless with in their writing. Today, we are going to focus our attention on the comma and the multiple ways writers use the comma to make their writing readable, engaging, and strong."

For this lesson, you will want to have an example text ready—either your mentor text for the unit or another student's essay, or even a published essay in the world—where the author uses commas in a few distinct ways. Try to find a text where the author uses commas after sentence introductions, to list adjectives or verbs, or simply to add on a descriptive or clarifying clause. Of course your students will not necessarily use this language, but you will want to make sure that you give the class a text that has at least these three comma usages, if not more, as in the below example:

Later on in the story, Bradbury uses the sun to symbolize all that the children of Venus do not have. The sun symbolizes warmth, happiness, and even play. As a symbol, the sun is in contrast to the rain, which is constant, gray, and deadening.

Show students the text and ask them to pay attention to the commas that they see. Remind them that commas serve different purposes for authors, and that it helps our writing to know what those purposes are. You might demonstrate thinking through the first comma, saying something like, "So the first comma I see is right at the beginning, right after the line, 'Later on in the story,' and I guess, well it seems like the author is using a comma there to show when something happened, almost to introduce the sentence." You might begin a one-day chart for your class to use in thinking about their comma usage. Many teachers have made a chart such as this one:

Why Authors Use Commas

- To say when or where something happens

Then ask your class to take a closer look at the rest of the paragraph, working with a partner to think through how each different comma is used. As the class works, you will want to move among the partnerships, coaching students to find language for the purpose behind the comma usage. It will be natural for your students to begin by simply noticing the commas and retelling where they are used, so your job here will be to push students to say what job those commas do in the writing. Here is a list from what students have commonly said after this lesson:

Why Authors Use Commas

- To say when or where something happens
- To list description words or details (usually in threes)
- To add more to a sentence, like a detail or a backstory
- In quotations

Remember, your goal here is not that your class necessarily learns the academic language for independent and dependent clauses. Your goal is that your students become more powerful writers, as quickly as possible. That being said, if after today's lesson you wanted to offer students the proper names for the moves they noticed, certainly these names will stick more once your class has actually engaged with the commas themselves.

After you have collected a few ways that authors use commas (like the chart above, though yours may be different) have your students go to their essay drafts to identify some places where they could try one of these moves in their own writing. If need be, you could demonstrate this quickly on your own essay, but there is no need to demonstrate if you think your class could run with the work without it. Have the class work with their partners to try out a few new comma moves and then to mark up the rest of their essays with places they could continue the work.

Since this is an editing lesson, you will want your link to encourage your students to pay attention to *all* they know is important when editing a piece of writing. Their work with the comma today should simply be added to their editing repertoire. You might carry the metaphor of doing dishes further here—urging them to identify a variety of things they may be careless with when they write, and having them set goals for the conventions they should be aware of as they edit their pieces today.

Some teachers have had their students write on top of their drafts a quick list of editing moves to pay special attention to; others have had their writers simply talk to their partners about what their intentions are. Either way, taking some time here to broaden their view of the editing work in front of them will help to keep your class focused on the bigger work at hand—attending to conventions in their writing.

CONFERRING AND SMALL-GROUP WORK

Your one-on-one or small-group work with students today will be best served if you have done even a little bit of research ahead of time. For today you will want to help students with editing support where they need it most. This is not the time to unfurl your pet peeve of *its* vs. *it's*. This is the time to truly help your students have more control over their writing. This will take a little bit of planning. How that planning goes is up to you.

You could collect some student work—either from this unit or the unit before—and take a look at what your students struggle with most when editing their pieces. When assessing your students' needs, be sure to focus first on those convention errors that most get in the way of meaning—what makes it tough to understand their writing. These are the most critical needs your students have (*its* vs. *it's* can wait). Once you have identified these needs, or if you are one of the lucky ones that can find nothing that makes it really hard to understand your students' writing, then you might move on to the likely long list of errors that get in the way of the voice, or the flow, of the writing. Setting these priorities is important as it allows you to pull groups based on need and to let students know the importance of learning to control these conventions.

If you do not have the time to collect student work, a day or two before this lesson you could move around the room while the students are writing, researching on the fly. While you will not be able to get a deep sense of what your students need, this more surface research is miles better than none at all.

Once you have your data, you can now gather these small groups together to help students where they are in their editing journey. You might choose to teach them a rule directly and ask them to apply it to their writing, or you might continue the inquiry work you began in the lesson. Whatever your method, your teaching will be that much more effective with research because it will match the students in front of you.

Today is a great day to "make someone famous." When you see one of your writers transform a sentence from a simple subject and predicate to something more interesting and powerful, all by using commas, stop the class and read aloud the before and after so that the whole class can hear what others are doing, and get a little inspiration.

Of course this work is best when the first student you make famous is not your most naturally talented writer. While your advanced writers should certainly get their days in the sun, it will be more effective if the students you highlight feel within reach of most of your writers. Celebrating their work feels like a celebration of everyone's work—you will find that this lifts the spirits of the class during an editing day and inspires the entire group to move forward.

SHARE

For your share today, explain to your class that tomorrow you will be moving on to a new kind of essay, but that before you move on, you want to give them a chance to clean up any loose ends in their writing so far. You might want to frame this work as having a "perfectionist's attitude." Many teachers have used sports figures or music producers as good examples of perfectionists in action. Recently one teacher discussed Tom Brady's postgame interview where he outlined all the mistakes he made—after a game where he won by two touchdowns. Explain to your class that this is a choice that only they can make—to try for perfection—and to decide what that means for their homework that night.

Point out all they can use to decide what is not yet "perfect" in their writing—at this point they have charts and checklists and models and their partners. Give your class a few minutes to decide what their homework will be that night, how they can work to make their writing more "perfect," and ask them to write a note to themselves that will remind them later on. Of course, their homework will be self-directed, so if you would like some accountability around their choices, have them also write you a note on a Post-it that tells you what their assignment will be. You might suggest an amount of homework, perhaps a time frame that students should be spending on their writing, and give some examples of appropriately sized plans, if your students are apt to over- or underestimate how much they can get done.

Know that in the next session you will be leading your class to dabble in a new kind of essay—the comparative essay. To set students up for this work, you will also want to ask them to bring in a text that they think would make an interesting comparison to the one they've been writing about. You might offer a few suggestions of texts you would bring in to compare with "All Summer in a Day" and purposely include a variety of forms in your explanation (novels, stories, poems . . .) as well as a few reasons for comparison (similar characters, themes, styles of writing) so that students are set up to look for more options.

Best wishes,
Kate and Katy

Writing across Texts

IN THIS SESSION, you'll teach students that literary essayists often write as a way to think about more than one text at a time, pushing themselves to do the work of comparing and contrasting similar ideas across different texts.

GETTING READY

✓ Texts students selected for the previous night's homework, to compare to the ones they have been working with throughout the unit. They will also need the texts they have been working with for the unit (see Connection and Active Engagement).

✓ Your own text ("If Only We Had Taller Been") selected to be a comparison text to "All Summer in a Day" as well as your copy of "All Summer in a Day" (see Connection and Teaching)

✓ Your own writer's notebook entry, comparing the two selected texts, enlarged for students to see (see Teaching)

✓ "How to Write a Thematic Essay" anchor chart, from Bend I (see Active Engagement) 💿

✓ "How to Write an Author's Craft Essay" anchor chart (see Mid-Workshop Teaching) 💿

✓ "Narrative Writers Aim Toward Goals Such As . . . " and "Narrative Writers Use Techniques Such As . . . " charts (see Conferring and Small-Group Work) 💿

✓ Your own comparative essay claim, enlarged on chart paper for students to see (see Share)

✓ Students' writer's notebooks and pens (see Share)

COMMON CORE STATE STANDARDS: W.8.1, W.8.7, W.8.9.a, W.8.10, RL.8.1, RL.8.2, RL.8.3, RL.8.4, RL.8.5, SL.8.1, L.8.1, L.8.2, L.8.3

Y OUR EIGHTH-GRADERS are comparing themselves all of the time, for better or worse. Think back to your own adolescence, and chances are that your thoughts were often hijacked by concerns over whether you were as good-looking as that kid, as smart as your lab partner, as talented as the star. Of course your wish for your students is that they would be a little bit easier on themselves, that they would love themselves a little more. But this stage of development is critical for their growth as adults—putting their own identities next to the world around them and wondering—how do I measure up?

In the next two sessions you will ask your students to use what they have learned about literary essay writing to compare and contrast two texts—one that they have read for this unit and one that they have brought in from home or your library that they think would be interesting to compare. This work leans on the fact that your students have written compare-and-contrast essays before—both in sixth grade as well as (most likely) every year they have taken a state test—and it also looks forward, to exams like the New York State Regents exam, in which students are often asked to write about texts they know so well that they can write about them from memory. Your state may differ in its expectations, but know that for many of your students the ability to write about a text you have read in the past is an important one, as is, of course, the ability to write a comparative essay.

This eighth-grade work raises the level of the work students have done in past years by taking work that was previously coached and supported and making it increasingly independent. You may have students who struggle with this independence. For example, your students may not bring in a text on their own, or you may worry that your whole class will simply grab any old comparison text to bring in—and it may therefore be a smart move to have some backup texts on hand that are likely to support this work—most likely short texts like poems or songs or very short stories that can be read in a flash. But even if you build this safety net, we encourage you to challenge your students to walk the tightrope without you. Very soon they will be in high school, and you will want them to have had the experience of figuring out which resources do and don't support their ideas, without the help of a teacher.

In this session, you'll demonstrate how to write-to-think about the themes in two different texts, encouraging students to reprise transition words and thought prompts from past teaching. Your demonstration will also remind students of the spirit of writing-to-think—speculation rather than blanket claims, exploring rather than prematurely proving. You will support students in naming themes in both texts before sending them off to work independently, collecting entries that explore their thinking across two texts. You'll keep that exploratory spirit alive as you encourage students to use partner talk as a resource to jog their thinking and keep their momentum high.

"Very soon your students will be in high school, and you will want them to have had the experience of figuring out which resources do and don't support their ideas, without the help of a teacher."

Writing across Texts

CONNECTION

Remind students of what they were asked to think about for homework, choosing a text that would serve well as a comparison to the one they have been working with throughout the unit.

"In the previous session I asked you to come in with a text you've read before that would be interesting to compare to the text you've been writing about in this unit—turn and show your partner what you brought and say a little about what made you think this would be an interesting comparison."

The class began to talk. As they did, I gathered the students who did not bring anything and gave them a few texts to choose from that I had selected. Once those students were reading through their texts, I addressed the class:

"I was doing this too—thinking last night about what sort of text I might compare with 'All Summer in a Day.' It was hard work! But I found something cool—it's a poem written by the same author—Ray Bradbury. Here is just a bit of that poem."

"If Only We Had Taller Been"

The fence we walked between the years did bounce us serene.

It was a place half in the sky where, in the green of leaf and the promise of peach, we reached our hand and almost touched the sky.

If we could reach out and touch, we said, it would teach us not to, never to, be dead.

We ate, and almost touched that stuff;

Our reach was never quite enough.

If only we had tallied then, and touched God's cuff, his hem

We would not have to go with them, with those who had gone before

Who, short as us, stood tall as they could and hoped that by stretching tall that they could keep their land their home, their hearth, their flesh and soul.

◆ COACHING

Some texts you could use for this purpose are songs like "Roar" by Katy Perry, or poems like "The Road Not Taken" by Robert Frost, or "Mother to Son" by Langston Hughes. Ideally, students will use comparison texts they're familiar with, so if there are songs, poems, or short stories that are especially popular with your students, and have some rich themes, you will definitely want to include those.

But they like us were standing in a hole.

. . .

I work for that.

Short man. Large dream. I send my rockets forth

between my ears,

Hoping an inch of Will is worth a pound of years.

"When I read this I sat up straight—I realized that this poem had a lot in common with 'All Summer in a Day'—not just because the same guy wrote it, but because of the ideas within each text—their themes."

❖ **Name the teaching point.**

"What I want to teach you today is that literary essayists often write to think and grow ideas about more than one text at a time, pushing themselves to do the work of comparing and contrasting similar ideas across different texts."

TEACHING

Name some steps students can take to generate writing-to-think about two texts.

"I know you've done work like this before—you have written compare-and-contrast essays. You'll try flash-drafting one tomorrow, but today I want to show you the kinds of thinking and notebook work you might do to set yourselves up. First, you will probably want to start with naming the themes you see in both texts, to give you a starting point, and then you will pick a theme to compare that feels kind of similar in both texts. Next, you'll definitely want to write long and use your writing to help you figure out what you're really trying to say. This means you need to draw on any tools or strategies you already know to keep yourself writing and keep your thinking flowing."

Set students up to watch your process as you compare themes in texts.

"Watch me go through these steps with my own texts—and look for the tools I'm using to push my thinking, because after I show you, I'll want you to tell your partner what I tried.

"Okay . . . so first I'll want to talk about the themes in both. I know that one theme, one I already wrote about, in 'All Summer in a Day' is that when people can't get over their own pain, they wind up hurting others. Hmm, . . . does that theme fit this poem? Let me reread it quickly now." I skimmed the poem a bit, shaking my head. "You know, I don't really see that theme here. But last night when I was reading this poem, I was thinking that one theme in this new text is that people often want what they can't have. Like how in the poem it says 'Short man. Large Dream.' The poem is about wanting something bigger than what we have. That actually feels sort of similar to 'All Summer in a Day'—so even though these texts are different in some ways, I think I can compare how they address this theme.

In this instance, I am choosing just a snippet of a poem, because I do not want to take the time to read a whole short story (or novel) with the class. If in your classroom you have already read a story or novel that would be interesting to work with, by all means use that text.

If you feel your students will need more support with using these steps, you could jot them on chart paper to provide students with a step-by-step To-Do list of sorts when they go off to write.

"The next step is to write long about how those themes seem the same and different in the two texts. Let me show you what I did, and you can study this to see what moves you might make in your own writing. Look for the things I'm doing to keep myself writing and to push my thinking." I displayed my entry to the class:

> **Both texts share the idea that** people sometimes want what they can't have, and that this hurts. For example, in "All Summer in a Day," the kids desperately want a break from the unending rain, but they don't believe it will really happen. **Similarly**, in the poem "If Only We Had Taller Been," the speaker wants to achieve something big, to explore the sky, but he's not tall enough. **This makes me think** that in both texts, there is a really intense desire for what you cannot have—you see what you want but you can't quite touch it. **I think that is a difference in these texts**—in "All Summer in a Day" the desire for what they cannot have makes the children mean, but in the poem this desire makes the speaker a dreamer, and kind of ambitious. **So now I'm thinking that what's true in both texts** is that in life, desperately wanting something you can imagine but can't reach can push you to do things you normally wouldn't do—either negatively or positively.

Guide students to debrief what you did to compare two texts.

"I asked you to look for what I did to try to push my thinking. Were there thought prompts or transition phrases you noticed that I used? Were there certain ways of thinking you saw evidence of? Tell your partner." The class began to talk as I coached in, saying things like, "Name the exact phrase I used," or "What kind of thinking did I do in the beginning and then at the end of this entry?" Soon I brought the class together.

"So, a lot of you noticed that I used some of the same thought prompts that you've used before, like 'This makes me think' and 'So now I'm thinking . . . ,' and I also used some transition words that are specific to comparison, like *similarly*. Many of you also noticed that I did some comparative thinking, that I discussed both what was the same in the texts and what was different about them. And a few of you even noticed that I pushed myself to change my mind and try out different ideas in my entry, not just sticking to the one that I first thought."

ACTIVE ENGAGEMENT

Get students started thinking about and naming the themes in their comparison texts.

"I want you to get a head start on this kind of thinking right now. Remember that before I compared themes, I had to name a few themes I saw in both texts, and then see which ones they had in common, where the overlap in ideas might have been. I know each of you brought in different texts to compare, but you can help each other to find the connections to the original text, the one you have been writing about so far. Try that with your partner right now. You already know a lot about how to talk about theme—if you need a reminder, I've put our 'How to Write a Thematic Essay' chart front and center again—check out that first bullet point!

This can be tricky for students—it's more challenging to notice small differences in how a theme plays out over two texts than it is to compare two completely different themes. In my demonstration notebook entry, I therefore try to be very explicit about what is similar and what is different, hoping to make this thinking crystal clear to students.

These are some of the key items you'll want to highlight for students from your essay—of course there may be others students see. As eighth-graders with a lot of writing experience under their belts, your students should take on as much of the responsibility for paying attention to and naming what they're being taught as they can. If students don't notice these or similar strategies, you will want to point them out explicitly rather than trying to prod students into saying what's on your mind.

> - Collect ideas about the themes in a text.
>   - Name a central problem or issue that characters in the story face.
>   - Reflect on parts of the story that pertain to this problem.
>   - Think to yourself, "What is this story teaching me about this problem, this issue?"
>   - Write long about your thinking to grow your ideas, perhaps by asking how different characters relate to that issue.

I listened in as students began to talk with partners. Antoine told Myah, "Okay, so I was already writing about *Divergent*, and then I brought in the second Harry Potter book! I read it a million years ago, but last night I was thinking about how in *Divergent*, it's all about how who you really are is not just random, it's a choice, except that the world tries to tell you who you are sometimes. And then I remembered how in Harry Potter, he wanted to be in Gryffindor, and it was chosen for him."

I leaned in, asking, "So you're thinking that a central issue in Harry Potter is choosing who you are instead of having it chosen for you?" Antoine nodded. I turned to his partner. "What can you ask Antoine to push him toward saying a theme?" Myah studied the chart and then asked, "So what does the author teach you about choices in Harry Potter?"

Recap what you heard, highlighting supports that will pay off for students.

After a few minutes I brought the class back together and said, "I heard a lot of you using steps from our old chart to figure out themes in the second story you brought in. I also saw some smart partner work, where you reminded each other of some thought prompts and thinking moves that might help you grow your thinking. I am so proud of the ways you are learning to help each other this year."

LINK

Encourage students to make a plan and move quickly.

"So, writers, you're off to a really good start. Think about the comparison work you need to get done today. Are you going to start by writing long? Do you need to look back at some earlier notebook entries? Which ones? Are there charts that will help you? Jot a plan box for yourself at the top of your page, then go off and get started right away. You'll want to work quickly, so that at the end of the period you have some solid thinking on the page—probably two pages of entries or so—about how you can compare these two texts."

Responsive Teaching through Small-Group Work

TODAY YOU'LL HOPE TO SEE a lot of attempts at comparison and a lot of notebook writing. Not all of your students' attempts will be successful on the first try, and you may see writers who had brilliant insights around theme struggle when they work to compare two texts. This is a great sign! Facing and learning from intellectual challenges will help students grow, and this is a challenge your students will be ready to try their hand at. This may be a day when it pays off to gather a few impromptu small groups, targeting your teaching to help students overcome some of their most common obstacles. As they set off to work, this is your opportunity to do some quick research into what your students are doing. Some teachers like to use the first few minutes of a workshop this way, perhaps jotting names onto a grid of possible small groups as they watch kids get to work and read a bit over their shoulders. Once you have a small group's worth of kids who need the same teaching, don't wait—dive right in!

One group you might gather will be students who are trying to force comparisons, perhaps because the texts they brought in don't quite work. You may see these students attempting to write particularly labored connections between two texts, ones in which the logic falls apart more than usual. Some of these students might notice this problem themselves, asking you for help. Teach this group that when their text selection isn't working, it's better to step back, rethink, and choose a different text (or a different claim) than it is to keep forcing a square peg into a round hole. The backup

---

MID-WORKSHOP TEACHING   **Comparing Craft as Well as Theme**

"Let me stop you all for a moment, because I am dying to tell you guys all about what Jonathan did. I was having a conference with him, and he was writing about the themes in his two texts. And then he said the smartest thing—he turned to me and said, 'So, we did that stuff before, writing about craft . . . I feel like I should be using that too.' Wow! Needless to say, I think that's a terrific idea—of course we want to use everything we know as we're working! Thinking about and comparing authors' crafting decisions is another great strategy to use when writing comparative essays. I'll share a snippet of Jonathan's work about craft with you to inspire you—maybe this is something you'll want to try, too. Here's what he wrote."

In "Harrison Bergeron," I notice that Kurt Vonnegut is using short sentences whenever the family is talking but then he uses long, fancier sentences when Harrison is talking. And in "The Knife of Never Letting Go" the author does kind of the same thing, because when we are in the head of the Prentisstown men there are these really long jumbled sentences. I think maybe Vonnegut is doing this to compare Harrison to everyone else in the story so we realize how different he is, but Ness is using his long sentences to show how confused and chaotic it is in the men's heads. So both authors use the same crafting technique, but they use it to show different things.

"Do you see how Jonathan is using some of those patterns we saw when writing about craft to help him compare and contrast? He explains a pattern he's noticing, then tries to figure out why the authors would each choose to create that pattern. I'm sure that some of you will want to try this—remember, you can always look back at the last essay you wrote, or of course our 'How to Write an Author's Craft Essay' chart to help you do that!"

In the book Twisted and A True
Diary of a part-time indian, both
characters, Junior and Tyler were both
looking for hope and change in A
True Diary of a part-time Indian, Junior
went to a new school to find hope
in himself because he wanted to be
something he thought white people had
the most hope so he switched to Rearden,
an all white school and left his tribe.
He changed after he went to the new
school, he believed in himself more and
found hope in himself. In Twisted, a
similar theme happened. Tyler was a
nobody who was in love with a girl
Bethany, he had no hope that he would
ever be with her, which wasn't true
because they did end up together and
throughout the book, he had the
courage to talk to her. Tyler was
always told what to do by his dad,
he never stood up for himself to tell him →

FIG. 15–1   Emma compares themes of hope and change in
Twisted and *The Absolutely True Diary of a Part-Time Indian.*

texts you prepared for those students who came unprepared can
be a resource for this group.

Another group you might find is a cluster of students whose
compare-and-contrast work is very surface level and mechanical.
You might see students jotting down themes that are far less
complex than the work they're capable of doing, themes like "Be
kind" and "It's good to be honest," just so they have some easy
points of comparison. Another way that this problem might show
up is when you see students who are listing similarity after similarity or difference after difference, as if the two texts are either
identical or diametrically opposed. With this group, you might
coach kids to talk longer with a partner, pushing each other with

thought prompts, to develop their thinking before committing it to the page. You may
also need to remind these students to draw on specific parts of past teaching. Maybe
some students need to think back on the teaching in this unit about theme (refer
them back to the first bullet on the anchor chart you referenced in today's minilesson),
while others need to think back to sixth grade, when they worked on comparing and
contrasting two stories.

Finally, you may also notice kids who are flying through this work in thoughtful ways.
It's often easy, in a busy and crowded classroom full of kids with a range of needs, to
overlook those students who need a greater challenge. But these students also need
to grow, and will benefit from clear, targeted instruction as much as anyone else. This
group might benefit from studying how two authors develop a similar theme in different ways, whether focusing on craft or structure. Use two familiar texts as an example,
either "All Summer in a Day" and "If Only We Had Taller Been," or two familiar short
texts from earlier in the year, naming the similar theme and launching a mini-inquiry
into how the authors reveal that theme. One way to set up this work might be to refer
to the narrative writing techniques and goals charts used in Session 9. You could invite

students to compare texts' development of the theme along different lines—does one author develop the theme through revealing character actions, while another relies on strong imagery? You could then encourage students to do some writing around this with their own texts, moving from student to student, coaching each one.

As you confer and lead small groups, you might put an emphasis, as you have in earlier sessions, on lifting the level of the writing, even in notebook entries. If you see students doing this—perhaps revising as they write to use more sophisticated academic vocabulary or going back through an entry, making their analysis clearer or stronger—this is something to acknowledge. It also might be useful to carry, as you confer, reminders for yourself of the most useful and powerful teaching points and conferences you've used throughout the unit; sometimes this can help you—and your students—recall the ways students have strengthened their writing before.

Writing a Comparative Claim

Set the stage for the work ahead—writing a flash-draft of a comparative essay.

"Nice work today! I have to say, when I make comparisons I always feels like I see all of these things in my texts that I never saw before—it's a cool feeling, and I hope you got a chance to feel that today. So, tomorrow—in one class period—you are going to write a whole essay where you compare the themes in these two texts. Don't worry! You may not realize this, but you pretty much have everything you need at hand; you know everything you need to know to write some pretty fantastic comparative essays. But to really be ready for that work, you are going to need an essay claim, and you will want to have a sense of how your essay might go."

Show students an example of a comparative essay claim and have them try one on their own.

"I want to pause here at the end of class and give you a chance to draft a claim before you leave. Claims for comparative essays are a little different from other claims you have written during this unit. Because you are addressing two texts, your claims may be a little longer. Here is a claim I could use for my two texts." I flipped to a sheet of chart paper, where I had written my claim.

> In both "All Summer in a Day" and "If Only We Had Taller Been," we learn that that in life, desperately wanting something you can imagine but can't reach can push you to do things you normally wouldn't—either negatively or positively.

"See how I start my claim by saying 'In both texts . . . we learn . . . ?' Try that out now, on your own, in your notebook. Write out a quick rough-draft claim now."

Record a few students' claims for the class to see as further examples for their own work.

"So here are a few I saw you drafting." I turned to the chart paper where I had listed my claim and began writing down a few of the claims from the class. "Antoine wrote 'In both *Legend* and *The Hunger Games* we learn that to survive, you have to trust people.' And Winnie wrote that '*The Maze Runner* and *Ask the Passengers* both teach us that not knowing who you are is the most painful thing to experience.'"

PREPARING TO FLASH-DRAFT

"Writers, tomorrow you'll be flash-drafting an essay that will rely on the work you've started today. So think for a moment about what it is that you'll need to do tonight to be ready for that. For one, I know you will need to have a plan for your essay, just like you did for the last two essays you have written during this unit—so tonight you will definitely need to make sure you have a strong claim, and that you have sketched out a plan for your essays. Right now, would you tell your partner what else you'll need to do to prepare? Then jot your assignment down in your writer's notebook, so that you are all set and ready to go tonight."

Session 16

Writing Comparative Essays on Demand

I T IS A TEACHER'S GREATEST DREAM. After teaching your heart out, after watching your students work hard, you see them sit down to take a test or apply what they have learned to a new situation, and they are able to adjust their knowledge to a new situation, deftly applying strategies you taught to slightly different tasks. You pump your fist in the air, Rocky style, knowing you have done your job well.

The opposite of course is a teacher's worst nightmare—teaching your heart out, watching students work hard, only to see blank stares and furrowed brows when a writing situation calls for similar, but slightly different, work. You want to scream out "You *know* this! You *know* how to write an essay!

These dreams most likely cause you to lose sleep at night. Your students will often be asked to write quickly, and time and time again as they get older, they will be asked to write in response to tasks that may not perfectly match the ones they've tackled in our classrooms. Part of your job, and a goal of this session, is to help students practice drawing on what they've learned so they can tackle new challenges.

Pushing students to stay focused and keep moving will be essential in this session. The Common Core writing standard 8.10 calls for students to "write routinely over . . . shorter timeframes (a single sitting or a day or two) for a range of discipline-specific tasks, purposes, and audiences." Whether or not your state is using the Common Core, you likely agree with the writers of the standards that being able to produce strong work on demand is important, and you want to see your students working with flexibility.

This session, like the previous one, sets students up to work with flexibility, concentration, and increasing independence. They will quickly review the qualities that make good essays, and take stock of all the resources they have available to them. Then they'll move into flash-drafting their own essay, and make a plan to continue working on it for homework. Throughout the session, much of your instruction will coach students to use strategies that they will also be able to use when you aren't there—like checking in with a partner, relying on resources they have on hand, and setting goals to keep moving forward.

IN THIS SESSION, you'll teach students that writers have to use all that they know about essays to write not just well, but also quickly and with flexibility.

GETTING READY

✔ Chart paper and markers (see Teaching)

✔ Grade 8 Argument Writing Checklist (see Teaching) 💿

✔ Students' writer's notebooks, folders, Post-it notes, and pens (see Teaching and Active Engagement)

✔ Texts that students are using to write comparative literary essays (see Active Engagement)

✔ Copies of model comparative essay (see Active Engagement) 💿

✔ Students' comparative essay drafts (see Share)

COMMON CORE STATE STANDARDS: W.8.1, W.8.4, W.8.7, W.8.10, RL.8.1, RL.8.2, RL.8.3, RL.8.4, RL.8.5, SL.8.1, SL.8.6, L.8.1, L.8.2, L.8.3, L.8.6

Writing Comparative Essays on Demand

CONNECTION

Tell a story that demonstrates that you having to draw on past learning to do something challenging. Connect this experience to the work students will undertake.

"So, writers, you did some powerful comparison thinking yesterday in class and last night. You knew coming in that today the plan was going to be for you to do a quick flash-draft of a comparison essay. When I was thinking about that last night, I remembered the time I was in high school, getting ready to take the SAT to get into college. I was completely freaking out the night before, just a mess. I told my mom, 'But I have no clue what the essay will be—I don't know what kind of essay to plan for! I just wasted all those long hours I spent learning stuff in English class!!!' I might have been just a *little* bit melodramatic, and I maaaybe even gave a *little* tiny eye roll.

"But my mom stopped me. She said, 'Wait, wait, wait, you definitely did not waste your time! When you do get to the test, you'll have a huge advantage. You know and have gotten good at so many different ways to organize your thoughts into an essay, so when you open the test booklet, no matter what they want you to write, you'll be able to figure out a way to structure it. The essay you are asked to write might not be exactly like the ones you have written before, but you know enough about essay writing to make it work, no matter what.'

"And you know, it turned out my mom's advice was totally right. I think I remembered that story last night because I was thinking about why it's so important for you guys to be doing this work. As you get older in school, one of the most important traits you can have is flexibility—the ability to adjust and problem solve no matter what is thrown at you."

❖ **Name the teaching point.**

"Today I want to teach you that sometimes, writers have to use all that they know about essays to write not just well but also quickly and with flexibility in a new situation, by quickly recalling what they know, assessing their resources, and making a plan to put their knowledge into action."

Though certainly the skill of writing flexibly on demand is not just a test-taking skill, the experience of having to write this way on a test is one that might resonate with lots of kids—and probably adults, too. Students may hear themselves in your teenage complaint and recognize the frustration of realizing that they aren't sure if their knowledge will transfer to a new situation—a frustration that you are about to alleviate.

TEACHING

Stress the importance of gathering all necessary resources and materials before beginning to write, to maximize efficiency.

"Anytime I want to do something and want to do it quickly, it's important that I feel prepared. Take for instance, when I'm baking a cake. I enjoy baking, but whenever I am trying to bake a new kind of cake I need to pause, think through what I am about to do, and get organized. I take the time to gather everything I need beforehand. I pull out my cookbook, and read through the recipe. And then I start collecting stuff. Flour, baking soda, sugar, eggs, vanilla, etc. I pull it all out of the pantry and line it up on the counter. And then on to the tools! I grab my mixing bowl, measuring cups and spoons, the whisk, a wooden spoon, anything I could possibly need to mix up my cake. Only then, when I have all of my ingredients and materials gathered, only then do I get to work. It's just so much easier to be well organized.

"Now, you know me well enough by now to know where I'm going with this." There were a few snickers, some murmurs among the class. "You got it. Writing a new kind of essay, especially a quick flash-draft essay, is just like baking a new kind of cake. You are all experienced essay writers. Not only have you already written two essays in the last month, but you have also written many more essays over the course of your middle school careers. And all of you have that essay recipe in your head. You know what you need. Today you are going to have the whole class period to write a compare/contrast essay about the claim you offered yesterday."

Ask students to reflect on the resources they have available to them.

"Take a moment to assess your resources. Glance around the classroom, flip through your notebooks and folders, talk to your partner. What are the tools and ingredients you'll need to have alongside you as you draft today?" I gave the students just a moment to talk, and then pulled the group together.

I turned to the chart pad and quickly jotted out the title "Ingredients and Materials for a Comparative Literary Essay." Then I turned to the class. "So, what do we need? I'll get us started. I would say I'd definitely want to have the eighth-grade Argument Writing Checklist at hand." I added the first bullet to our chart. After a few minutes of conversation, we had generated a comprehensive list of essay ingredients.

Ingredients and Materials for a Comparative Literary Essay
- Argument Writing Checklist
- Annotated mentor texts
- Books or texts that are being compared
- Writer's notebook

The details in this anecdote help to engage students in the lesson. Just as specific details make writing come to life more than general overviews do, it often helps make lessons memorable when you include specific images.

This baking metaphor is one of the many examples of occasions when teaching writing skills feels a lot like teaching life skills. You'll undoubtedly find other times when this is true, and feels like an opportunity to embrace. To be successful in college, careers, and life, your students will need writing strategies, and also strategies to organize their thinking, their resources, and their time.

- Classroom charts
- A strong claim
- Old essay drafts
- An essay plan
- Writing partners

"Okay, so we have a good list of what we are going to need to get our compare/contrast essays going today, but not everyone is going to need the same thing, so get ready to make some choices."

ACTIVE ENGAGEMENT

Channel students to make a plan, thinking about what they will find most useful as they write.

"There are a few things on this list that I think you already have. We talked about claims yesterday, you drafted some at the end of class, and you were supposed to firm those up for homework last night. You were also asked to sketch out a plan for how your essay will go. So I'm assuming you all have a claim and a plan that you are ready to work with." I did a quick assessment by glancing around the room, noticing which students were looking a bit sheepish, and making a note to myself to get to them as soon as the class went off to work.

"Once I send you off to draft, I want you to be fully prepared. Just like I have all my cake ingredients and materials lined up and ready to go, for maximum efficiency, you need to do the same for your essay writing. So I want you to get started, right now, and name the resources you think will help you the most, listing them out with a partner. Go ahead—and remember to help each other remember any tools that you might be forgetting. I am going to be looking for you to actually point to the charts you will use, and to make sure you have the checklists or mentors that you will need. Go ahead!"

Argument Writing Checklist

	Grade 8	NOT YET	STARTING TO	YES!
Structure				
Overall	I laid out an argument about a topic/text and made it clear why my particular argument is important and valid. I stayed fair to those who might disagree with me by describing how my position is one of several and making it clear where my position stands in relation to others.	☐	☐	☐
Lead	After hooking the reader, I provided specific context for my own as well as another position(s), introduced my position, and oriented readers to the overall line of argument I planned to develop.	☐	☐	☐
Transitions	I used transitions to lead the reader across parts of the text and to help the reader note how parts of the text relate back to earlier parts. I used phrases such as *now some argue, while this may be true, it is also the case that, despite this, as stated earlier, taken as a whole, this is significant because, the evidence points to, and and by doing so . . .*	☐	☐	☐
Ending	In the conclusion, I described the significance of my argument for stakeholders, or offered additional insights, implications, questions, or challenges.	☐	☐	☐
Organization	I organized claims, counterclaims, reasons, and evidence into sections and clarified how sections are connected.	☐	☐	☐
	I created an organizational structure that supports a reader's growing understanding across the whole of my argument, arranging the sections to build on each other in a logical, compelling fashion.	☐	☐	☐
Development				
Elaboration	I brought out the aspects of the argument that were most significant to my audience and to my overall purpose(s).	☐	☐	☐
	I incorporated trustworthy and significant sources and explained if and when a source seemed problematic.	☐	☐	☐
	I analyzed the relevance of the reasons and evidence for my claims as well as for the counterclaim(s) and helped the reader understand what each position is saying. I made sure all of my analysis led my readers to follow my line of argument.	☐	☐	☐
Craft	I intended to affect my reader in particular ways—to make the reader think, realize, or feel a particular way—and I chose language to do that.	☐	☐	☐
	I consistently used comparisons, analogies, vivid examples, anecdotes, or other rhetorical devices to help readers follow my thinking and grasp the meaning and significance of a point or a piece of evidence.	☐	☐	☐
	I varied my tone to match the different purposes of different sections of my argument.	☐	☐	☐

Sum up students' work, focusing on independence.

After a minute, I reconvened the class. "Writers, it was great to hear so many of you talking about all the different tools you'll be using, the charts and checklists and mentor texts, laying out all of your 'essay ingredients.' You know where these resources are in the room—and anyone who isn't sure where to find something that you need, you'll want to check with your partner before you go to work. You should all have copies of the old mentor text in your folders, the theme-based essay that I wrote. I have another mentor text for you to look at if you think it would be helpful, a comparative essay. I'll put copies of that one each of your tables."

LINK

Build energy around working hard, but purposefully.

"So you're going to want to work really, really hard today. This unit is nearing its end and you want to be able to say you finished strong. Your job today is to push yourself to draft a comparative essay—at least the body paragraphs. Just like my mom advised me in high school, this will be a time to use everything you've learned to write quickly as well as powerfully. Take a moment now to look back over the notebook entries you wrote in the previous session, and when that work feels fresh in your mind, go silently off to work. You've got this!"

It will help, not just today but all the time, to have clear systems in place for students to access resources. Some teachers find it useful to have folders for their current unit, perhaps stapled to a bulletin board or in a specific drawer or shelf space. These folders might contain extra copies of mentor texts, old student work, or checklists. While you could flood these folders with resources, students will probably use these more successfully if you are selective and mostly include resources you've introduced to the class.

Coaching on the Run

TODAY YOU WILL PROBABLY FIND you have many varied needs to address in your conferring and small-group work. Since you're near the end of the unit, though, you also will have many resources to encourage students to draw support from. This day is a great opportunity for you to make sure that students are identifying and internalizing the strategies from this unit that work for them. As students work today you will do less pulling of small groups and more on-the-run coaching. Since time is of the essence on any day, but particularly on a day like this when students are flash-drafting, you may be reluctant to interrupt students for a full-fledged conference if they are hard at work. However, you can accomplish a lot with lean prompts—imagine yourself as a running coach, pulling alongside a runner for just a brief time, offering encouragement as well as suggestions, before fading back to let the runner put your coaching into action. Some of the coaching tips or voiceovers to the whole class that you might use frequently today include:

"Don't forget to use the model essay!"

"You're going back to the texts to use exact quotes—well done!"

"Which charts could you use to find a reminder of how to do this work?"

"I can see you're starting to elaborate on one of your ideas. Remember the kinds of evidence you could rely on!"

"Don't stop—part of this work is to keep going, from one part to the next."

> In *The Name of the Star*, Rory discovers that she can see ghosts. A spring of murders pop up near her location in London that are just like the Ripper murders from over 100 years ago. In addition, Rory thinks that the killer is a ghost who is after her. An example of when Rory forges her own path is when she is going to face the Ripper once and for all with her ghost seeing/fighting friends Callum and Stephen. In the book, it says "I have to go with you," I said... "Not a chance," Stephen said quickly. "We're hiding you somewhere along the way. You don't have a choice," I countered. "Neither do I. He wants me. He's going to come after me. And if you fail, he's going to get me eventually..." "Let me put this another way," I said. "I'm coming. I'm not asking permission. I can't live like this. I can't live not knowing how this ends," Rory shows here how she is forging
>
> her own path. She went against everything Stephen said to her knowing that she may not come back alive. Just like Eden, Rory shows bravery and and courage in her own way by facing her problem head on. Just as Eden sacrificed everything for his nation and himself, Rory does the same for herself. She took control of the situation, made her own decision, and took a risk by choosing the hard way out. All actions do have consequences though and Rory was lucky that her sacrifice paid off in the end. Clearly, these two books have this same theme about forging your own path running through them and their characters share many similar traits. While these two books are very relatable, they are also very different when comparing them to this theme.

FIG. 16–1   Alec uses quotations as evidence of the theme of "forging your own path" in *The Name of the Star*.

You'll have noticed that several of these prompts suggest that a student is already doing the thing you might want them to do. It's often helpful to name and support the smallest gesture toward a strategy, as this can give a student confidence that he is, indeed, on the right track, and put a name to a technique that he will likely now use over and over again.

MID-WORKSHOP TEACHING   **Stop and Take Stock**

"Writers, freeze for just a moment. Take stock of where you are right now—what resources have you been drawing on? What's working well so far? What do you think you're leaving out of your work? One way you can take stock is to check in with the mentor essay I gave you—how is yours looking in comparison? Is there anything you noticed that I did, that you could incorporate into your essay to make it stronger? You have about fifteen more minutes of writing time today and you will want to use it well.

"Talk to your partner for just a minute, to refocus yourselves and set a goal for your remaining writing time."

A Symphony Share

Set students up to share powerful sentences they've written that day.

"Writers, first and foremost, well done. In just two days, you've put together some really strong writing comparing two texts, which can be tough work. I'm impressed. Let's set ourselves up so that everyone else can be impressed too. We're going to do a symphony share—where I point at you and you call out a line from your piece. Right now, everyone pick out one line you think is pretty powerful. Pick fast!"

After just a moment, I continued. "We'll be in silence, and when I point to you, say your sentence. Ready?"

I conducted the symphony, keeping the pace up so there was just a breath of air between students' lines.

SESSION 16 HOMEWORK

TAKING IT FURTHER

"Tonight, for homework, I want you to make some more progress on this draft. There are a few different possibilities. You might want to draft an introduction and conclusion for your essay. You might want to go back and do some really focused revision of the work you've done today. Or maybe you feel like there's a part of your essay you want to redraft, because you're not happy with how it went. Decide right now, what is your plan for tonight that will help you get this flash-draft as far as it can go? Don't forget to write down what you decide!

"You know that at this point in the unit, we are getting ready to celebrate. One of the things that writers do when they are feeling pretty good about pieces of writing is to think about who to share it with and where to share it. Tomorrow that's going to be our big focus . . . sharing and publishing and celebrating. So tonight, look back over your whole body of work in this unit. Take home your notebook and all your drafts, and spend some time reflecting on your work. What have you learned? What have you gotten really good at? And, biggest question of all, what audience might be particularly interested in what you have to say? Come in tomorrow with some of this thinking done."

Publishing on the Internet

ear Teachers,

Congratulations! You and your writers have come to the end of a rigorous, intellectually demanding unit, one that asks a great deal of all of you, but one that also gives mightily in return. As you know, it is so important to end our units of study with a proper celebration, a way of rejoicing in the work accomplished and skills learned. In addition, it is equally important that students see their writing go out into the world, authentically, as often as possible. If writing is seen simply as assignments completed and given to the teacher for grading, then many of your students will not engage with their own writing identities, for writing will not hold enough meaning for them. By connecting the work they do in your class to the real world around them, you allow students to see that writing is a powerful medium to put their ideas out into their communities.

That being said, it is quite a challenge to find the authentic and celebratory ways to end a literary essay unit. After all, you do not see many flyers for "Literary Essay Readings" at your local coffee shop, and rare is the best-selling "Book of Lit Essays" displayed at your local bookstore. It will be tempting for you to give your kids a high-five, collect their essays, and move on, avoiding the very real need to make this work relevant to them. It is, however, possible to do so, and well worth the effort it entails.

All it takes is a simple Google search for a popular Young Adult novel title to see that the Internet is chock-full of powerful (and not so powerful) writing about reading. As the seventh-grade unit *Writing About Reading* highlighted, young people all over the world are taking to their computers to publish their opinions and passions for the texts they are reading. As this unit comes to an end, your students have a collection of work around one text—why not help them to see the ways that they could offer their thinking to the community of people who are already in conversation about the texts they have studied?

Have your students decide where on the Internet they will publish some of their thinking about the text they have written about. Most likely they will not publish their entire essay, and in fact they will probably revise a touch to strike the right voice for a website.

COMMON CORE STATE STANDARDS: W.8.1, W.8.5, W.8.6, RL.8.1, RL.8.2, RL.8.3, RL.8.4, SL.8.1, SL.8.6, L.8.1, L.8.2, L.8.3

Your students could choose to write a comprehensive review on Goodreads.com, or they might go to the fan page of a popular YA book and comment there. Perhaps they could start their own blog—either as a class or around a certain title that a few students read—posting their essays on the blog and then publicizing to gather followers and commenters across the globe.

As you ready your students to publish on the Internet, you will want to give them a few tips to be sure their writing is Internet ready. Teach your class that:

1. Internet ready means edited *perfectly*. Usually bloggers will have at least two people read their posts to look for errors before publishing.

2. The Internet is often not as formal as the classroom. Try revising a part of your essay (or writing a new post from scratch) that is a little less formal. Decide who you are speaking to—if it is fellow teenagers, you could use language they might recognize (as long as it is appropriate). While you still want to sound as smart and sophisticated as you can, certainly you can strike a more conversational tone when you publish online.

3. As a writer on the Internet, you should be ready to have a conversation. The joy of the Internet is the community you can find there. When you post your insights about a text, people may respond— agreeing or disagreeing. Check in every few days and see if people have commented on your post. Remember that the best conversations are civil ones, so even if you are annoyed by what someone says, treat them with respect online—just as you would in person.

As your students choose where to publish and work to get their writing out into the world, you might reserve your tech lab or iPod cart for a day of celebration. Bring punch and pie and have your writers load the site where they posted, allowing the class to walk around, seeing the action, and commenting when they have something to say. Some teachers have set a standard that during the celebration students should comment on at least three posts by their classmates.

For your final moment, before moving on, gather your class around. Let them know again how proud you are of their work, and how much the path of this unit will help them in the years to come. Ask your class to share one thing they will take with them into the future, the next time they are asked to write about texts. Go around in a circle, or call on kids symphony style, and relish the sound of the goals they have set for themselves, in the deep footprints of your teaching.

Best wishes,
Kate and Katy

They say nobody controls their own life. If you don't think for yourself, you can't be your own person. In _Ender's Game_ by Orson Scott Card, Ender learn what disasters can strike if you don't think for yourself. You could be killed, or even become a killer. You could find yourself agreeing with the things you always hated. You could wake up and find that WWIII is taking place right outside your bedroom window.

Ender doesn't know when to think for himself. He just goes along, playing the games of the government officials until he can't take anymore. Then he does what he thinks is right. But unfortunately Ender doesn't always stop in time. In Command School, he just goes along, playing games on the simulator, not realizing that his simulated battles are real until too late. Too late to save the billions of innocents (Buggers(aliens)) he slaughtered on the "simulator." I know that Ender was being controlled when on page 160, Colonel Graff says, "That Demosthenes and Locke aren't as under our control as _the Wiggin_." This means Graff believes Ender (_the Wiggin_) is under his control. If Ender had noticed this, he might not have wiped out the Buggers.

Valentine is becoming her own worst nightmare. She has been going along, playing the twisted games of her older brother Peter, helping him by writing to change the world under the pseudonym "Demosthenes." But Valentine knows that Peter only wants to keep the world in one piece, because he thinks it'll help him dominate it

faster. Valentine knows this, and so she can avoid being drawn into her brother's temptations... right? After writing Demosthenes for years, Valentine is able to know what he would say without Peter's consent. She even finds herself _agreeing_ with what she writes as Demosthenes, while finding the things Peter writes with the pseudonym "Locke" weak and close-minded. I know that Valentine wasn't thinking for herself when she started agreeing with Demosthenes because, on page 163, Val thinks, "Perhaps it's impossible to wear an identity without becoming what you pretend to be." This means Valentine thinks that she is _becoming_ Demosthenes, agreeing less and less with _herself_ as she begins to agree with her counterpart and opposite.

To sum it all up, be yourself. You should never let yourself be controlled by someone else, no matter what. Though the consequences won't always be as bad as they were for Ender, they won't be good. You might be like Val, and start agreeing with the things you always hated. Val, who lived 3000 years before she felt she had done enough good to settle down and raise a family. But the point is, you never know what will come from not being your own person, and you don't want to find out. So always think before you do something, _am I choosing to do this? Is this the right thing to do?_ You'll know the difference.

FIG. 17–1 Lucas' final essay

Alec   Compare and Contrast Essay

In our modern world, almost every step you take from birth to death is watched. You progress and grow to bigger and better things throughout your lifetime, thus becoming better with each of those little steps you take. Those small steps lead to bigger steps and eventually, you will have left a path behind for your successors to follow. What sets some people apart from others is that those who don't decide to follow that path forge a new one and thus change everything. Without people who were different, and who kept striving for greatness even though they were told they couldn't or shouldn't do it, our world would be nowhere near as advanced as it is today. People like Martin Luther King Jr., The Wright Brothers, Nelson Mandela, and countless others throughout time who chose to lead a different path. To quote the great poet Ralph Waldo Emerson, "Do not go where the path may lead, go instead where there is no path and leave a trail." Only you can decide what lies ahead and by "forging" your own path, you control where that path will lead. In other words, you should not let others control who you are or what you are going to do, rather you are the ultimate authority in your own world. In the books Champion and The Name of the Star, several characters lead their own paths, make their own decisions, and change everything.

In Champion by Marie Lu, the main character Day has lost everything. His mother, father, and one of his brothers are all dead and he can't love his "girlfriend" June because she a constant reminder of his family. He also has a disease in which he was told by the doctors is going to kill him in the next month or two. His brother, Eden, is the only thing he has left and he constantly struggles to watch and protect him at any cost. Long story short, it is about 100 years in the future and America as we know it has split into two combatting nations, The Republic, and The Colonies. An epidemic is spreading like mad throughout the colonies and they will attack the Republic if they do not provide a cure. The only catch is that the Republic doesn't have a cure. Eden does have a disease that is similar to the colonies current outbreak and the Republic wants to get Eden from Day so they can run tests on him, find a cure, and save the "world." These tests can't guarantee Eden's complete safety though and this hurts Day more than anything. He can't bear to

lose the one thing he has left that he loves in Eden. So being the protective brother that he is, Day says no and keeps the Republic away from Eden. Day even threatens to have the people revolt if they try to take Eden. Everyone, from Day to the government has a say in this except for Eden himself. Finally, when Day tells Eden about the whole ordeal, to his surprise, Eden agrees to go through with the tests. In the book, Eden says this to Day "I remember what the Republic did to us. Of course I do. But the colonies are invading. I want to help... It's my decision to make. Not yours." Eden shows here that he wants to help the Republic by putting his life at risk. He went against everything that Day said to him, but in the end, Eden made his own decision and did not let others sway that decision. He set an example of courage and bravery by making his own choices while forging that new path. All while displaying exemplary character which you must put faith in order to achieve such success. This theme is also on display in The Name of the Star by Maureen Johnson and can thus be compared to Champion.

In The Name of the Star, Rory discovers that she can see ghosts. A spring of murders pop up near her location in London that are just like the Ripper murders from over 100 years ago. In addition, Rory thinks that the killer is a ghost who is after her. An example of when Rory forges her own path is when she is going to face the Ripper once and for all with her ghost seeing / fighting friends Callum and Stephen. In the book, it says "I have to go with you," I said... "Not a chance," Stephen said quickly." We're hiding you somewhere along the way. You don't have a choice," I countered. "Neither do I. He wants me. He's going to come after me. And if you fail, he's going to get me eventually..." "Let me put this another way," I said. "I'm coming. I'm not asking permission. I can't live like this. I can't live not knowing how this ends," Rory shows here how she is forging

FIG. 17–2   Alec's final essay

her own path. She went against everything Stephen said to her knowing that she may not come back alive. Just like Eden, Rory shows bravery and and courage in her own way by facing her problem head on. Just as Eden sacrificed everything for his nation and himself, Rory does the same for herself. She took control of the situation, made her own decision, and took a risk by choosing the hard way out. All actions do have consequences though and Rory was lucky that her sacrifice paid off in the end. Clearly, these two books have this same theme about forging your own path running through them and their characters share many similar traits. While these two books are very relatable, they are also very different when comparing them to this theme.

In both Champion and the Name of the Star, the characters often lead their own paths. What makes those journeys' different though, is the way in which they forge those paths. Even though Eden and Rory each have their own individual storylines and problems that they solve, they address those problems in different ways. Eden does not know the situation he is in until Day tells him. He then makes the decision to go through with the surgery and claimed that he had been thinking about it. Since he is young, Eden doesn't get told everything, especially things that are very important. He is "shadowed" from the world in a sense, especially because of his illness and that definitely gives Eden the rebellious courage to go through with the surgery. It's almost reverse phscology in the sense. Eden is younger and was unaware that he may have been forced to take the tests. That made him want to take the tests even more and prove everyone wrong. Rory on the other hand knew the full background regarding her situation and she knew every little detail about the killer she had to eventually face. In addition, Eden is doing this to help his country while Rory is doing this to save the city of London where the story is set. They are both doing this to help themselves as well.

In life, there is always a choice. Always a path. You can either follow the paths already made by your predecessors, or you can choose to create your own path. Even our everyday lives, for example, do you get the same piece of candy as your friend to look cool or do get the one you really want? Do you choose to smoke because others around you are too? Your path is one that only you can make and over the course of your life, you will either follow the path of others, or forge one that is your very own. In both of the books previously mentioned, the characters had to deal with a problem and faced it head on. They both displayed tremendous amounts of courage and bravery while clearly forging their own paths.

FIG. 17–2   (continued)

SESSION 17: PUBLISHING ON THE INTERNET   153

In the book Matched by Ally Condie, Cassia Reyes is the main character. Throughout the story Cassia has many struggles and problems. The author uses many crafts to reach her goals.

One goal the author uses is to build empathy for Cassia. Cassia met a boy named Ky Markham. They started to talk more and more each day. They got so close they fell in love with each other. But she is not alowd to pick who she wants to love. She was match by her best friend Xander, but she told him it's not going to work. If you do such a thing, and switch your match you could become an aberration, which is almost like an outcast. When the officials found out about their secret relationship they got into big trouble. They were also sent away for a while so they can think. But Cassia really missed Ky. On page 363 Cassia thinks to herself, "I think of him, I think of him, I think of him." Cassia is thinking this so the reader would build empathy for her. The author did this so the reader would feel the pain of loosing someone she loved. This is how the author uses many crafts to reach a goal.

Another goal the author uses is building and setting up a problem for the next book in the series. When Cassia got sent away she never stopped thinking about Ky and trying to find him. The whole time she was away she remembered things that Ky either told her or wrote her on his pictures. On page 365 Cassia remembers what Ky wrote to her, "Cassia. I know which life is real one now, no matter what happens. It's the one with you." This is setting up a problem because Ky is telling her that he loves Cassia. But they can not talk to each other or see each other because they are way to far away. Cassia really wants to see Ky and Ky really wants to see Cassia. The author makes a cliff hanger about where Ky is. Cassia wants to go on a journey to find him. The author made the end of the book like this so the problem will lead into the next book. Cassia and Ky might never see each other again but to them that like death. This is how the author used another craft to reach a goal.

FIG. 17–3 Lara's final essay

In many novels written by the notorious Patrick Ness, there are many dashes to cut a sentence short, and most sentences only have three or four words in them. Why, you may ask? There is a reason for everything and this is not any sort of grammatical error... there is a purpose for this. Patrick Ness' craft that he uses to write his illustrious novels consists of short sentences, and ideas cut short by a dash, just to be so called "forgotten", but as Patrick Ness introduces a new idea, the last one seems to linger through your soul, begging for answers, trying to figure out what is going on. One thing that is common in Ness' novels is that the protagonist is often trying to piece the world together with the reader, as seen in More Than This.

Patrick Ness' use of dashes and short sentences in his novels truly brings a mysterious element to the book and it is a neat way to get the reader stirred up, hoping that they can figure out what was going to be said. For example, Patrick Ness uses this craft on page 20 in More Than This,

"But that's impossible. He hasn't seen this house, this country, in years. Not since primary school.

Not since —
Not since his brother got out of the hospital.
Not since the very worst thing that ever happened.
...
This is hell.
A hell built exactly for him.
A hell where he would be alone.
Forever.
He's died, and woken up in his own, personal hell.
He vomits."

In this quote, Patrick Ness cuts many sentences short and suddenly stops in the middle of a huge concept. The reason for this is to make the reader think, What exactly is going on? This also shows that the protagonist, in this case, Seth, was trying to piece together bits of information with the reader. Patrick Ness has a unique style of writing and that is what gets the reader hooked on his books. Ness uses short sentences in order to show that the protagonist is trying to piece together the world around him. For example, in the previous quote on page 20, Seth is beginning to piece together bits of his life, he is just starting to figure out the truth, but when Seth is on the verge of getting some answers, the sentence stops. This shows how abrupt his life really

FIG. 17–4 Rachel's final essay

is, his brain is like a train riding through Crazytown, his whole world seems like a dream-like blotches of memories forming into a cloud of mystery. The reader develops a gaping void in their soul when Ness stops in the middle of a sentence.

Another example of this craft is on pages 174 and 175 of <u>More Than This</u>,

"It's so close, so close he could dash out of here right this second and run up it —

...

To the edge of the sheer cliff.

They stopped him.

In the nick of time.

And he considers this, too.

A boy and a girl, appearing from nowhere, stopping him just before he started up the hill, just before he met the black van.

Which also appeared from nowhere.

Did he call them into being?

Did he make them arrive?

Just in time?

But Tomasz and Regine. Preposterous names, foreign, even here.

And the van. And the Driver.

What was that all about?"

In this scene, the protagonist, Seth, is battling to find out the truth. Patrick Ness shows this battle by asking many questions that were going through Seth's mind. Ness also included many short sentences in this scene. This shows that Ness is trying to gain the reader's interest. In this particular quote, Seth was seconds away from re-committing suicide because he felt so isolated in the screwed-up world he had just entered. Patrick Ness shows Seth's isolation, fear, and confusion through questions and short sentences. The way that Ness suddenly stops his sentences shows how the character is feeling baffled as he has just entered an incomprehensible planet that he cannot understand. The way that the sentences sound makes the reader envision Seth wide-eyed and perplexed, with his mouth hanging open. This is a great way to get the reader to create a picture of the character in their mind, and to imagine how awestruck he must be feeling at this moment. Patrick Ness does an amazing job of getting the reader to feel empathy for the characters as he drags them into another world.

As you can see, Patrick Ness has a unique craft that is used in his bestselling novels. Ness' use of dashes and short sentences are in his books for the main purpose of interrupting the reader's train

FIG. 17–4   (continued)

of thought so they could think about what is actually going on. When the sentence suddenly stops, the reader wants to fill in the missing parts with their own ideas. This is a well-known technique in his novels and it serves well in getting the reader to analyze and interpret the text. It is important for the reader to understand what is going on in the book and Ness makes sure of this by breaking down the text into short, to-the-point sentences. Patrick Ness could truly influence and inspire other writers to use this technique.

FIG. 17–4   (continued)

Most people are influenced to follow popular beliefs and traditions. In "The Lottery" by Shirley Jackson, the townspeople all support the common tradition of the lottery. In "Harrison Bergeron" by Kurt Vonnegut, most people do not believe in competition and support handicaps. Both authors use mood and dialogue to suggest that just because the masses follow a common belief or tradition does not mean it is right.

Shirley Jackson uses mood throughout "The Lottery" to show that just because the masses follow a common belief or tradition does not mean it is right. The mood undergoes a great shift at the very end of the story when the author reveals the purpose of the lottery. With just a few lines, the author is able to manipulate the text to feel morbid and haunting. The narrator writes, "'It isn't fair, it isn't right,' Mrs. Hutchinson screamed, and then they were upon her" (5). The mood, which is light and airy for the majority of the text, becomes innnediately twisted, deranged, and contorted. When the author shifts the mood, the readers can finally see how wrong the lottery is and the negative effects of blindly following others. In modem-day society, stoning people to deatq is considered to be wrong and illegal. In the community of the story, however, it is a popular action because it is an old tradition and no one questions it. This shows that a belief or tradition can be innnoral even if it is popular.

The mood undergoes a similar shift in "Harrison Bergeron" when the glimmering fantasy of Harrison's empire is shot down, which further develops the theme. The formerly triumphant, celebratory mood becomes sorrowful and melancholy at the end of the story when Harrison is shot after giving the performance of a lifetime. The narrator states that, "It was then that Diana

FIG. 17–5   Aisha's final essay

Moon Glampers, the Handicapper General, came into the studio with a double-barrelled ten-gauge shotgun. She fired twice, and the Emperor and Empress were dead before they hit the floor" (351). The above change in mood is the turning point in the story where the author most strongly conveys that the laws of equality can result in the occurrence of brutal, wrong events. By using words such as, "double-barrelled ten-gauge shotgun," and "dead before they hit the floor," the author was able to create a dramatic and grotesque mood. This displays the theme that just because the masses follow a common belief or tradition does not mean it is right When Harrison, who represents sheer genius, marvel, and wonder, is shot, it brings the reader to the conclusion that competition is beneficial because it allows people like Harrison to succeed.

In "The Lottery" the author develops theme by using dialogue that shows the townspeople's attitudes towards the lottery. While the townspeople wait for the lottery to begin, one person mentions that some other towns had gotten rid of their lotteries. This, however, is not a popular idea in the village the story takes place in. Old Man Warner responds by saying, "Pack of crazy fools... there's always been a lottery" (3). From this, the reader can infer that the townspeople continue the tradition of the lottery only because it has been going on for as long as they could remember. The villagers blindly fo i si ustom, although it is inhumane and they have forgotten the reason it started in the first place. By including the dialogue between townspeople, the author was able to show the common attitude towards the lottery, which makes the theme apparent in the story.

Dialogue is also used by Kurt Vonnegut in "Harrison Bergeron" to develop the theme that just because the masses follow a common belief or tradition does not mean it is right. In the beginning, George Bergeron's wife, Hazel, proposes that he take off his handicap, but George

thinks this is not a good idea. George explains, "1fl tried to get away with it... then other people'd get away with it- and then pretty soon we'd be right back to the dark ages again, with everybody competing against everybody else" (3). When George says these words, his belief in handicaps becomes clear. By including everyday dialogue in the Bergeron household, the author is able to replicate a scene that seems typical between husband and wife during that time period. Knowing what the common belief is in "Harrison Bergeron" helps develop the theme of the story.

Throughout each of their short stories, the authors of "The Lottery" and "Harrison Bergeron" use literary devices such as mood and dialogue to show the theme. Both Shirley Jackson and Kurt Vonnegut suggest that popular beliefs and customs are not always morally correct. In both stories, the masses believe in something that would be considered wrong and unpopular today. Shirley Jackson writes of a flawed town that blindly follows old tradition, while Kurt Vonnegut writes of a dystopian society that bans competition. Each story implies that if people are brave enough to think independently and stray from popular beliefs, then civilization can thrive.\

FIG. 17–5   (continued)